STEP BY STEP

By the same author

Invitation to the ballet
Come dance with me

STEP BY STEP

The formation of an establishment

Ninette de Valois

W. H. ALLEN · LONDON
A Howard & Wyndham Company
1977

Printed and bound in Great Britain by
Butler & Tanner Ltd, Frome and London,
for the Publishers, W. H. Allen & Co Ltd,
44 Hill Street, London W1X 8LB

ISBN 0 491 01598 4

ACKNOWLEDGEMENTS

I would particularly like to thank Miss Mary Clarke, editor of *The Dancing Times*, and Mr Clement Crisp for their invaluable help and advice.

I would also like to thank Mr John Tooley, the general administrator of the Royal Opera House, Covent Garden, for his kind permission to reproduce my Memorandum; and the editor of the Journal of the Royal Society of Arts for his kind permission to reproduce The English Ballet: A Lecture to the Royal Society of Arts.

The Publishers would like to thank the following: the Executors of the Estate of C. Day-Lewis for their permission to reproduce an extract from *The Poetic Image*, published by Jonathan Cape Ltd; Penguin Books Ltd for their permission to reproduce four lines from '*People*' by Yevgeny Yevtushenko from *Yevtushenko: Selected Poems*, translated by Robin Milner-Gulland and Peter Levi, 1962, translation © Robin Milner-Gulland and Peter Levi, 1962; George Allen & Unwin Ltd for their permission to reproduce four lines from 'After the Storm' by Boris Pasternak from *Fifty Poems*; The Hogarth Press and Virginia Woolf's Literary Estate for their permission to reproduce an extract from '*How It Strikes A Contemporary*' from *The Common Reader*, 1st Series; David Higham Associates Ltd for their permission to reproduce from *The Poetry of W. B. Yeats*; The Bodley Head Ltd for their permission to reproduce '*Reflections*' from Alexander Solzhenitsyn's *Stories and Prose Poems*; John Murray Ltd for their permission to reproduce an extract from *Ruskin Today—An Anthology* by Kenneth Clark; and Victor Gollancz Ltd for their permission to reproduce an extract from a poem by Alasdair Maclean.

For Michael Somes

CONTENTS

PROLOGUE

The Wonder Children

(This article first appeared in *The Spectator*,
London, January 24th, 1964)

A picture of England before the First World War, a kaleidoscopic vision of seaside places, small county towns and Sunday
train journeys. . . .

As a girl between fourteen and fifteen years of age I was a
member of a group of child players; the theatre posters
announced our performances under the title of 'The Wonder
Children'.

We appeared nightly on the seaside pier theatres of England
and occasionally trod the boards of little nineteenth-century
theatres in the smaller county towns—they were invariably
named 'Royal' and they are today replaced by cinemas invariably named 'Regal'.

It is not difficult for me to recall that springboard sensation
one experienced when hurrying along the gas-lit pier deck.
There were the romantic moonlit nights with a twinkling shore
in the distance, then the dark tempestuous ones when we
battled through wind and rain to reach the theatre at the pier's
extreme end, with nothing to look forward to but that theatrical
depression of depressions—a 'poor house'.

Our stage settings were supplied from the theatre's 'stock'

1

and they never varied. There was always a crude palace scene backcloth, a florid landscape garden, and a set of tired, shabby black velvets. In a tiny orchestra pit would be found four orchestral players, a replica of any teatime restaurant ensemble in the town. They were prepared, though, to tackle the 'classics' with only an upright piano, two violins and a 'cello.

How were twenty children organised, disciplined and looked after? We all came from the same Theatre Academy in London, and the principal of the Academy was the lady who ran the show—elegant, shrewd and of Austrian origin. She was strict but much liked by us all. Her sister, who was a singer, toured with us and graced a secondary hotel in each town, whose marble steps we occasionally ascended to be either praised or scolded by this lady.

There was, however, a more dynamic force in our midst: a professional general-manager-cum-stage-manager. A member of the Association of Touring Managers, he knew all the answers. He was proud of the fact that he 'took out' *Peter Pan* every year, and would tell us of the splendours of a No. 1 tour. Dapper, efficient and kind; neatly dressed and equipped with a soft Homburg worn at a rakish angle; the picture was completed with a silver-knobbed walking-stick and yellow chamois gloves. With dexterity he would slip from the prompt corner (once the show was under way) to check the box-office takings; this was a move that met with my secret approval as I felt it was tied up with the safety of my £4 per week salary.

The domestic scene was also happily, if haphazardly, organised. A certain number of obliging aunts, cousins, mothers and spinster elder sisters came along with the 'Wonder Children' and looked after any little Wonder who was impoverished in the family line. We had no wardrobe mistresses and we had never heard of professional dressers. Each young Wonder packed and unpacked her theatre basket, mended and washed her theatre clothes; she was hooked, unhooked and quick-changed by one of the dedicated chaperones.

Nightly I danced my way through about eleven numbers.

2

Dimly I remember a very odd Hungarian dance, heightened by a resplendent pair of red boots. On I ploughed through *The Butterfly Ballet* (a red admiral), *The Dance of the Flowers* (a violet), to the great culminating effort of the evening—*A Children's Revue: Impressions of Famous Artists*.

It was here that I came into my own: I was Pavlova and danced *The Dying Swan*—dying twice nightly on all the coastal piers, for my 'death' was always ferociously encored.

All the performers under fourteen had to obtain a performer's licence—and go to the magistrates' court every Monday morning. On a return visit to one particular town the magistrate asked our manager which was the little girl who had danced *The Dying Swan*? I was over fourteen and therefore not present. Yet I was elated when I heard, for I had a Peter Pan-ish dislike of growing up and managed to look very young for my age. I also reflected with some satisfaction that he must have seen the show and remembered me. Then there was the little old lady at Eastbourne who came to the stage door every time that we visited the town to tell me: 'I shall look out for your name in the papers, the London papers. It will get there.' In this case I merely hoped. ...

Were we often tired? Certainly. Bored? Never. Quarrelsome? Rarely. Homesick? Guiltily aware that it was not the case. Jealous? Guiltily aware that it was the case. Frustrated? The word had not yet crept into our limited vocabulary.

Touring before 1914 swept you into a theatre life that was very complete in itself, and this awareness had its own form of snobbishness. There were first, second and third class tours; first, second and third class companies, and first, second and third class lodgings. There were great provincial stars who never deigned to grace London with their presence, and distinguished West End stars who were always expected to take to the road for many months with their latest London success.

The well-remembered, numerous and homely theatrical 'digs'; strictly classified, of course, but in all cases cosy and home-like. Whatever the grade, they offered comforts unknown today; I recall the coal fires and remember with relish the hot suppers actually cooked by the landlady after the show. Living cost just under £1 per week for everything.

The first week in August, 1914, found us appearing at the South Parade Pier, Southsea. The evening performance on August 3rd was one of tension and restlessness.

The next day war had burst on us. I stared at my supper plate that evening and a sympathetic ballet-mother asked what was worrying me. 'I want to know,' I said firmly, 'who is fighting with whom and against whom and why?' The answers were vague, hesitant and unconvincing.

It was the end, I knew, of the 'Wonder Children', but that worried me not at all; for on that memorable day a certain Wonder Child had, as such, already ceased to exist.

INTRODUCTION

Why the formation of an establishment? Why not just the story of the Royal Ballet? The answer is that the whole structure of the venture was deliberately planned to become one of those much derided pieces of architecture known as an Establishment.

The Royal Ballet was never meant to be an isolated personal effort in a particular highly specialised direction. It was to become something that would have a root in the country's theatre; something that the fully-fledged from within its walls might leave to spread their wings elsewhere, and again something to which they could return with their findings, and once more serve and sense the traditions from which they had sprung.

But what happens to the Establishment when the birds leave the nest? Nothing. It is too busy nursing the next group of fledglings.

Every tree has a root that produces a trunk. The trunk has branches, and the branches have twigs, leaves, buds and blossoms.

Great stars in the world of ballet today, however much they are rebels, travellers, or box office record breakers, are the children of an Establishment that somewhere, at some time, has lavished years of care on them and their development, and it is a fact that all these stars seek, throughout their freedom-seek-

5

ing careers, moments of glamorous respite and refreshment under the auspices of an Establishment.

The first part of this book gives a kaleidoscopic outline in three phases of the Royal Ballet's institutional development. The last part contains a series of impressions that directly or indirectly bear some relation to the former.

The contents do not have to be read in the sequence that they are written. Each phase represents a passage of time.

The reader may make his own choice.

PHASE I

The 1920s and the 1930s

The 1920s and the 1930s

In retrospect these years are the most significant in my career. It was a time when my mind was overflowing with schemes, ideas and plenty of frustration. Waiting from 1926 to 1931 for the completion of the new Sadler's Wells Theatre was the most frustrating ordeal of the lot.

In the early years of the 1920s I moved from the world of opera, ballet, variety, musical comedy and pantomime to the stately Diaghilev era. Yet another venture awaited me when, in 1926, I found myself involved in the English and Irish repertory theatres: the Old Vic, the Festival Theatre, Cambridge, and the Abbey Theatre, Dublin.

By January 1931 I was installed at the Sadler's Wells Theatre, and there commenced the greatest adventure of all.

Everything still demanded foresight; optimism was a ceaseless effort towards the stabilisation of all things great and small. However green the furthest field, there was always present the task of noting the shade of the field that we were all actually standing on.

Islington of the thirties with its pre-war background of poverty and neglect ... were we fortunate to be there? Very; and the longer I live the more obvious does it seem to me.

Here are some writings, old and new, that are relevant to the period.

9

THE TRAVELLER
A pupil and her teachers

... I leave the foothills of the images
and climb. What I pursue's not means but ends.
You may come, if you've a mind to travelling.
Meet me at the point where the language bends.
Alasdair Maclean

As a traveller who has never found lingering on the way the answer to an aim, I have managed to travel my way through three great schools of teaching. It was these encounters that helped the aim of the journey; I cannot dwell on an 'end', because in art there is no such thing.

I speak of the French, Italian and Russian Schools, not through those institutions that are devoted to their maintenance and preservation, but through lengthy contacts with great professors springing from such roots. Reactions in such cases are very personal and much concerned with the relationship between pupil and teacher, therefore it may well be that some artists who have found themselves in similar circumstances may disagree with some of my views.

It has often been my experience to notice that outstanding teachers show a tendency to fall into two main streams, those who boast that their students cannot succeed without them, and those who feel they have only succeeded if their students are so equipped that they can further their studies under any other

10

good teacher. In other words, the former wish to dominate a student's life, but in the case of the latter, self-reliance and adaptability are encouraged.

I was fortunate, as all my distinguished teachers left me with sufficient confidence and curiosity to probe afresh. It did not take me long to discover that their principles eventually merged; they did not cancel each other out leaving one in a world of bewildering contradictions.

THE FRENCH SCHOOL

Edouard Espinosa

I studied with this maestro from 1914 to 1917. When I think about his lessons my mind goes back to his specialised approach when teaching, for his was essentially the mind of a pedagogue. Reasoning and clarification played an all-important role in the proceedings.

His terminology is still the basis of the English technical school, and I can say with conviction that I do not know of any other that is superior—it is all based on extremely logical thinking.

Edouard Espinosa was the son of a great artist—Leon Espinosa; the father had spent most of his career in France, but he was also in Russia and attached to the Imperial Ballet at one time in his career. Later, Sir Henry Irving engaged him to help his actors and actresses in gesture and movement, and to assist in the Lyceum Shakespearean production. It was this engagement that brought a change in the family fortune, for Leon Espinosa and his entire family came to settle in England. One evening during the war Edouard Espinosa told me an amusing story concerning the Irving engagement. It appeared that Edouard was the member of the family who first met Irving and suggested that the great actor-manager needed his father's services. Edouard had been sent to London by his father to 'find a job for himself', but he returned empty-handed to Paris. 'Do you mean to say,' exclaimed an enraged father, 'that you have not got a job?' 'No,' said the son, hastily, 'but I've got you one.'

I worked with him three times a week, and my studies were divided into two half-hour private lessons and one class. We were also set examinations on theory and we had to make a complete study of the technical terms in relation to his peda-gogy. The lessons were very quick, with much *terre à terre* work. He excelled in the old French school of *petit batterie* and *pirouettes*. His footwork was extremely strengthening, but *adage, ports de bras* and big steps of elevation played a smaller part in the lesson. It could be said that much too much was crammed into the half-hour private lesson. But it must be taken into account that a dancer's life over sixty years ago in England knew little or nothing of the slow state school training in other countries. Well-spaced years of regular study were curtailed because of the uncertainty of work, training was spasmodic on account of the necessity of accepting any engagement offered in the theatre.

On my return from a lesson I would write down all that I had learnt in full. It was then carefully sub-divided into two courses of study with the execution slightly extended. These studies were practised on alternate days for about two hours at a time, for long hours of careful construction had to be worked out as no real advancement could be made on only two and a half hours' tuition per week by itself alone.

His musical approach was very precise and professional. He always knew the time signature that he required for either a step or an exercise and was also an adept at changing it, thus varying the rhythm of the step.

Espinosa's basic knowledge and approach represented a lot of very traditional old French school, and by doing so it naturally included some of its weaknesses. As an example, there was at that time the notable dilemma of faulty stance. This was not helped by the fact that we had to wear small foreshortened corsets. These bony structures gave an exaggerated curve to the

12

spine. His care of feet, ankles and knees was superlative. We were never allowed to go home in ordinary walking shoes; we had to wear laced or buttoned boots so as to support the ankles and keep them from swelling. (A few years ago Dame Margot Fonteyn told me that when she first wore modern boots after a class she felt far less tired, and she remembered that I had once told her about Espinosa's ruling.)

Although Espinosa was a *demi-caractère* dancer, he had brilliant *batterie*, an excellent old classical style when demonstrating in class and a very good '*ballon*'. Somehow he never managed to pass the latter gift on to his pupils; and I feel that the omission was due to the brevity and speed of the general training then in vogue in England. He had obviously had a much slower formative training himself, which had no doubt started some time in his sixth or seventh year. A good '*ballon*' definitely needs slow development.

He had some terse gnomic slogans:

'When you beat an *entrechat*, think of the *back* foot coming to the *front*.'

'Your head is the heaviest part of your body—control it.'

'When you pirouette, your eyes leave the audience last and come back first.'

'Do not force your instep, develop it slowly, and never put any pressure on the toes in a *battement tendu*.'

I owe, or rather owed, the eventual strength of my foot-work entirely to his careful schooling. When I first went to him, at the age of sixteen, I had my 'point' shoes taken away from me and replaced by soft shoes for a period of four months. I was told that it was done 'to get my feet placed correctly before I would not have any feet to place'. Four months in soft shoes for a girl who had danced *The Dying Swan* on almost every pier in England was a frustrating experience. The feet were saved, as perhaps was proved later when, at one time in the Russian Ballet, there were marks allotted by older members of the Company for various virtues (or lack of them) among the younger dancers. I received ten out of ten for my 'feet'. Again, at one time when my progress was slow and there were signs of a lack of stamina, Espinosa consoled my mother by saying, 'If the physique fails her the brain will take over.' Fateful words in later years when the physique did fail.

Much of his work is still to be found in this country, and if he were teaching today, in this more leisurely way of working and thinking we now experience, I feel sure that more benefit would be derived from certain aspects of his knowledge freed as they would be of the necessity to cram a student by means of studies that were too highly concentrated, and producing in the end in everyone a tendency to strain.

He bequeathed what we might perhaps regard today as too severe an approach to the pedagogy of the dance, but nevertheless, however much it is now curtailed the whole of it is worth an occasional scrutiny—whatever may be the artist's basic school training. His mark on the English School is to be reckoned with, in spite of the developments of today or tomorrow, and the writer regards herself as one of his many grateful pupils.

THE ITALIAN SCHOOL

Maestro Enrico Cecchetti

I joined Cecchetti's class in London in the spring of 1919 when he was in England with the Diaghilev Russian Ballet. It was my first experience of attending a class every day in the week. The studio, or rather hall, that we worked in was without mirrors and situated in the premises that housed the London 'Bolshevik Party' of those days. Our grim little dressing-room was known to be frequented by rats at night.

The class, and there was only one at that time, consisted of about ten students. I can recall among them Marie Rambert, Molly Lake, Ursula Moreton, Margaret Craske and Errol Addison. Lydia Lopokova came sometimes to our class, but in general she had private lessons. I would slip in to watch her working, and I have a vivid memory of the Maestro coaching her in a solo in the finale of *Boutique Fantasque*, for the ballet was at that moment in its early stages of production.

The classes were, at first, a terrible ordeal for me. I was always a very 'slow study', and a change of style and approach was an agonising experience. The situation was not made easier by the fact that the early summer found me dancing in a London 'revue' and also appearing in the first post-war international season of opera at Covent Garden.

During the month of August all the members of my class left London for a vacation. I was unable to get away as the revue was still running. Tentatively I went to the studio during the first week in August fully expecting to find it deserted. But no; in the otherwise empty studio there sat Maestro and Madame Cecchetti in a splendid state of isolation, doggedly awaiting some sort of pupil. I was hailed with much enthusiasm, and there and then started up three weeks of the most wonderful private lessons. Daily these lessons unravelled for me all the mysteries of his teachings that my slow thinking had not been able to fathom amidst the confusion of the general class and my heavy summer schedule.

Gone were his rather alarming outbursts of temper—the throwing of the stick along the ground at clumsy feet, the shrieks of 'aero-plane' when arms and legs in the general flurry lost all sense of symmetry and harmony. His enthusiasm, his kindness, his shrewd observations on my balletic virtues and vices made each day a treasured memory for all the years to come. In the background Madame would nod her head with approval and give me her encouraging smile.

The Cecchetti method is too well known to discuss in these pages. Like all 'methods' not the whole of it is for everyone, but the more important aspects are undoubtedly for the entire ballet world. I think that Pavlova's observation was very shrewd: 'Learn the Cecchetti method and then forget it.' She meant by the remark, of course, that the mind and the body assimilates what it requires and feeds every movement with this

15

need, and so unconsciously the new knowledge is absorbed into the work of the artist as a whole.

I do think that the method is important to study at some time in one's career, but perhaps not sufficient on its own. Other schools can be found which are more diffuse, less autocratic. The Cecchetti Method (as taught in the days of the Maestro) stated its case and one had to take it as a whole, without question, nor for that matter would there have been any persuasive answers. I would say, on reflection, that the many set exercises, heavy long *adagios* and systemised *enchaînements*, in the end appear to be more rewarding for the male dancer than the female. This is understandable as Cecchetti was a great executant, and the structure of his approach bore some resemblance to the Danish Bournonville School. August Bournonville was also a great dancer, teacher and choreographer who was said to be more successful with the male dancer than with the female—and certainly his sytem has had better results with men even to the present day.

In spite of Cecchetti's influence on the Leningrad School at the end of the last century, it is my opinion that this great Italian virtuoso was very influenced by his Russian contacts. It was there that he most surely learned to appreciate the aesthetics of the ballet. Italy, in spite of his great triumph there in *Excelsior*, could never have done this for him. His long association with Diaghilev as the Company's teacher and 'mime' further developed his understanding. Therefore, the mime roles, choreographed first by Fokine and later by Cecchetti's own pupil Massine, added another dimension to his work in execution. The association in general gave him a great tolerance and a wide appreciation of the qualities of various Russian ballerinas. He worshipped Pavlova, and that alone, from such a virtuoso of the Italian School, was very revealing.

I have heard, in my own Diaghilev days, groups of Russian artists discussing him and they were, on the whole, fairly objective. Yet through these very arguments I was always struck by the fact that the artists concerned were falling into one of

16

three groups: in other words they had either gone along with him the whole way, a little of the way, or none of the way. All their findings struck me as being equally plausible—a case of *chacun à son goût*. I always came away from such discussions quite sure that everyone was right—from the point of view of their own instinctively sought out searchings and findings.

He had many strong views and principles and, in contradiction to all that I say here, he always stuck to his view that 'no one should ever change their school'. It is true that one cannot change the deep-rooted fundamental approach, your body is tied to this by force of habit and development; yet you can explore the general scene and find answers to certain physical weaknesses that are not so well dealt with in one traditional school as they may be in another. After such experiences you return to your own roots considerably fortified.

The Maestro was wise and I treasure some of his remarks: 'A dancer must have a highlight to become a ballerina, she must have either exceptional elevation or strong "points" or good pirouettes.' But nevertheless he put 'grace' before everything in a woman dancer. He would say there was no such thing as a ballerina under twenty-six, yet there was nothing more beautiful to see than an embryo ballerina in her teens. He objected strongly to the extension of the height of the leg above the conventional 90°. 'A ligament is like elastic, if you stretch a piece of elastic it becomes longer—but it also becomes weaker.'

We had no pianist for our lessons. He deftly whistled his way through class accompanied by the tip-tap of his cane. We had a fixed tune for each particular step or exercise and this tune was whistled week in and week out. To execute *battements frappés* every day for three years to the overture from 'William Tell' tried my loyalties rather severely towards the end.

Many still regard him as the greatest teacher of the first thirty years of this century. I could never wholly favour one great teacher, for teaching is too complex a matter; so much depends on the fluctuating scene of pedagogy, the discoveries of one school or an academic temporary loss of confidence in another.

17

Again a variety of great teachers are needed for the individual needs of certain dancers.

The first two years of study with him was an illuminating experience, the last year a falling off—for I seemed to have reached a form of monotonous repetition that had no revealing highlights or unexplored side-tracks. The close daily study for two years had brought me to saturation point. Nevertheless, it is necessary to realise that it was only possible to reach this state in two years if you were, when you started, a dancer of some experience and technical knowledge. My remarks would not be applicable today to a student in his or her early teens.

The classes during the last year were very crowded, and Maestro was much taken up with getting the general routine pattern of each class passed on to the newcomers. I fear that the rest of us settled down into a groove. It had certainly taken some time to reach such a stage, and one readily admits that there had been a great deal of hard work on the way; nevertheless complacency now became one of the dangers.

I can still visualise the framed pictures on the wall of his studio depicting our weekly classes. There is a further remembrance of Maestro with his little watering can sprinkling the floor before class, and time and again he would rise from his chair to firmly close a window that had been opened by a perspiring pupil. 'You have to get warm to make your muscles work,' he would say. 'Why cool them off and labour in vain?' The room was often stifling.

From Cecchetti I learnt the meaning of symmetry, the hidden beauty of the studied detail, the harmony that can be achieved in movement and the meaning of *ports de bras*. He was very much the artist-teacher as opposed to the pedagogue. It was all a question with him of relative values. He further convinced me that a great teacher must live up to his own convictions, it is the pupil who eventually must get the whole into perspective, and in strict relationship to his own physical and intellectual approach.

18

As a final word I would say that I have always felt that he was an ideal professor for young choreographers to study with, and by far the best teacher for the artists of the Diaghilev period of the 1920s. Massine was a devoted pupil, and undoubtedly in the end his choreography was more understandable and easier to execute for those who had studied with Maestro Cecchetti.

THE RUSSIAN SCHOOL

Nicholas Legat

With the departure of Cecchetti in the spring of 1923 I found myself, within a week, at Nicholas Legat's classroom somewhere in the north of London. It was a spectacular change of scene, and once more I reacted to it in my usual state of nervous confusion.

Legat gave what were called in those days 'classes of perfection', that is the 'master class' of today. A 'master class' is a lesson given to those whose routine need of correction is over, they are classed as ready to attend the daily lesson as dancers of some professional knowledge.

Legat never left the piano; seated there he accompanied us with skilful and inspiring musical improvisations, he explained to us by word and by gesture the arrangement of the step or exercise, but remained seated at his piano. Only if a request had been badly misunderstood, or a dancer was in need of special correction, did he rise and come into the centre of the room.

Many found his method lethargic and his lack of detailed correction and systemised classes worrying. I found him an inspiring and lovable teacher. On me, a quick tense dancer, the Legat 'School' soon worked like a sunbath. After the first two or three days of application I found myself so stiff that I actually had to stay away for a short spell.

I remember gloomily sitting down to work out this problem,

for I was dancing three times a day in a show at the Alhambra and could not afford to get too tired. After a day or so I realised what had caused the trouble. I had executed, for over three years, routine exercises, *adagios* and steps that, in spite of their excellence and their technical demands, had become a mechanical set of movements that my limbs, body and brain had long absorbed. The strength that I could display in these well-known arrangements had now become irrelevant and had left me at this later stage without the necessary new surge of energy to accept at once the challenge of a changed order of things. Hence the stiffness, for I was unable to adapt, and became very strained trying to overcome the difficulty.

But in spite of the setback the subtlety of the lesson did not escape me; from the beginning I could feel the deep knowledge behind the elegant but apparently free and easy approach, highlighted by the everlastingly new and very beautiful *enchaînements* arranged from day to day.

Fairly quickly I fell in with the new pattern of work and I was soon made aware of expansion in my movements and experienced a new form of a more fluid strength enter my body. Just as I had seen certain Russian dancers respond with success to the Cecchetti Method (because it was what they needed), I responded to the Russian School for the very same reasons. It was going to make me a far stronger and more relaxed dancer.

Master and student in this case had a natural *rapport*, and as I improved I could feel that his interest in me increased. But after a few inspiring months my work was cut short as I was joining the Russian Ballet. I only had short sessions with him from then on, although I had him as a guest teacher at the Sadler's Wells Theatre during the early years.

He was, above all, a teacher who gave you a sense of existing in your own right, and never as an automaton for him. The sympathetic musical accompaniment had a great deal to do with this sense of independence. He had great powers of observation which went far beyond the mechanics of the dance.

In his well-known cartoons of dancers there can be seen shrewd observation, a personal comment on some highlight (or lowlight) in the artist's personality. I certainly found with him a path that extended my work, and I became more attentive to the importance of a more expansive expression in my classroom movements—valuable tuition for me, brief as it alas proved to be.

Madame Nijinska

If Nicholas Legat's conventional 'master class' lessons of the old Russian tradition were my first introduction to this school, the second, Madame Nijinska's classes, showed me the same basic work, but developed and extended beyond its conventional source, because her choreographic ideals and tendencies were to be interwoven into our daily class. She had theories that she considered we needed to study. It was not enough for us to accept them just as part of her choreography.

I was lucky to have the Legat experience first, it was as if I had studied the alphabet of a language carefully before I moved forward to a complex form of writing evolved from it. Madame's classes were interesting but difficult. Again I found them strengthening and in no time I noticed an improvement in my elevation. With her I had, as my second experience with the Russian School, a choreographer-teacher opening up my mind and strengthening my body. She was obsessed with correct breathing and gradually one saw the important relationship between breathing and movement. Correct breathing soon became a habit, so much so that it is now difficult to recall the theory involved that she would expound at great length. She taught us a very definite approach to body movement, as intricate as any contemporary dance, but strictly in relation to the classical school.

Exciting as it all was, and illuminating as far as her dance creations were concerned, it was a mistake to give us these les-

21

sons every day. Two or three times every week, with good conventional Russian School in between, would have been the perfect arrangement; alone it became wholly woven with her own special approach to choreography.

There was a 'deputation' to Diaghilev, and one stately lady of the older school told me that she had worn a cold compress on each knee—I presume to heighten the drama of the situation. Diaghilev did not appear to be unduly moved by either the deputation or the cold compresses. I was anyway enjoying this new approach to a class, and realised that it was all closely related to the ballets that we had to execute for her. I was young and looking for new ways of thinking, and I had already begun to feel a deep interest in choreography as opposed to mere execution.

Madame Nijinska was good to me. She taught me her own, very much re-choreographed 'Finger' variation in *The Sleeping Beauty*, coached me in the pizzicato of the same ballet's third act *pas de trois*, and even worked on me in *Red Riding Hood*. She rehearsed me carefully as Papillon in *Le Carnival* and, last but not least, plucked me from the *corps de ballet* of *Les Biches* (it was in rehearsal prior to its first production) and mounted her role of The Hostess on me. I was to be ready to show it to her when, after the general production was finished, she would be able to work on it for herself.

So it turned out that in addition to her classes full of body movements that I had never experienced before, I not only had her approach to both Petipa's and Fokine's dances but I had the privilege of having her theories further worked out on me in her famous role of The Hostess. Those long evenings spent in the rehearsal room—after the day *corps de ballet* rehearsals—are not easily forgotten; just four of us, Nijinska, Woizikowski, Zverev and myself.

Madame Nijinska was my first experience in the Russian School of a choreographer-teacher, and she proved to be a very great influence on my future outlook. I studied the Russian School in these specialised circumstances for eighteen months, and then Nijinska left us; but she left one inspired young artiste behind whose whole outlook was now beginning to take a very different view of choreography and the ballet.

There was though, even during this particular period of time, one more Russian School influence at work.

Olga Preobrajenska

The Diaghilev Ballet spent a great deal of time throughout the year in Paris; all our rehearsal periods in fact were held there once we left Monte Carlo.

During the visits four of us, Nikitina, Chamié, Doubrovska and myself, would arrange to spend one hour of our two-hour lunch break taking a special lesson with Madam Preobrajenska. She had been a ballerina with a famed technique and was a favourite pupil of Cecchetti when he was in Petersburg. Her approach as a teacher was strictly academic and equally rewarding. Here, in spite of the same traditional background as Legat and Nijinska, was a totally different personality at work. Her main distinction during her career had been her fabulous technique, and her teaching underlined her skill and common sense in her technical approach and further showed an understanding of the human material confronting her. She would note the case that needed a serious fault eradicated, and again would just as shrewdly encourage and develop a marked ability in any particular direction. Help was her aim, and in the speediest possible time. I well remember her acute power of observation. During my first few lessons she noted certain weaknesses in my left leg that I always went to great lengths to hide. We discussed the matter, and I was filled with gratitude as she nodded her head and said, 'I will help you here.' She did. (It was two years later that a London doctor told me that I had had polio in the leg as a child.)

I was, as usual, at first bewildered yet fascinated, so I held myself back for a few days and just endeavoured to take everything in; I did not attempt to dance full out. After a few days of tentative trial and error I let myself blossom forth along what I felt to be the correct lines. She came up to me one morning and said very quietly, 'I see; you wait, you watch, you make up your mind and then you work. This is a very very good sign.' I was staggered, as I thought that I was about to receive a reprimand for the way that I had held myself back. In no time she recognised that I was a Cecchetti pupil. She was one of the few Russians that I had met lately who had admired him wholeheartedly, and who had absorbed from his method what she wanted for her own dancing, and yet continued to teach her own basic school.

They were great technical lessons. At the end of my first series of them we went on a tour of Germany. I felt a different dancer on the stage, and I know that during the tour I danced better than I had ever danced before and, for that matter, afterwards. Her lessons represented the last act of my Russian saga, and seemed to bring my technique to its final point.

I returned to her studio whenever we were in Paris. She was very often refreshingly positive. I remember the day that she asked the three of us to execute our *Sleeping Beauty* variations as she wanted to coach us in them. I had to dance Nijinska's rearrangement of the 'Finger' variation. At the end there was a moment's deadly silence—then, *'Bizarre, très bizarre'* was the grim comment.

I would say that of all the great ballerinas teaching in Paris at that time Preobrajenska's classes were the most sound. This does not necessarily mean that she was everyone's choice, but outstanding among them all was her great and pure teaching; she was a very intelligent woman devoid of any unnecessary embellishments.

Thus I place on record my cross-section of Russian tuition that lasted just over a period of three years. Pure academic style and schooling with Legat, a choreographic approach with new slants on the teaching from Nijinska, and lastly the brilliant and shrewd technical approach of Olga Preobrajenska.

24

During those years I learnt to appreciate the cool calculated attitude of Russian artists to any change of tuition. There is, or certainly was at one time, a notable difference in the acceptance of Russian and English dancers to such changes. The Russians appeared to me to have an extroverted form of self-reliance more to the fore. Their minds were filled with a robust curiosity and their reactions based on practical self-preservation. 'What are we going to get out of this teacher?' seemed to be the unspoken question. It was often the reverse with the more reserved, introverted English dancers; there was a humble submission to fate, and the question was more like, 'What will this teacher be able to get out of us?'

There is only one way to learn, and that is by whole-hearted submission at the moment of learning. Only that way will your future personal reckonings succeed in being objective, and of true value in the final overall picture that you propose to frame and hang on the wall of experience.

THE FORMATION
OF AN ESTABLISHMENT

A Recipe for 'Establishment Pie'

Take equal quantities of knowledge and imagination.
Mix until thoroughly blended. Season with discrimination and roll out firmly. Bake in slow experience.
   Suitable for all seasons; can be served with varied
fillings, hot or cold.
   In the right temperature will keep for any length
of time.

Life at 'the Wells'

It was in the year 1931 that London witnessed the revival of
life at 'the Wells', for on the heights of Islington amidst the rattle
of the old London trams a theatre rose once more. It was built,
as everyone had hoped, on the foundations of the eighteenth-
century Sadler's Wells Theatre.
   The theatre was under the direction of Lilian Baylis of the
Old Vic. She had promised me four years previously that the
plans I had submitted to her for the formation of an English
ballet would come under her protection when the Sadler's

26

Wells Theatre was rebuilt. I just waited and did what I could to help at the Old Vic. I never had any doubts, for it all seemed to me a perfectly logical development that only asked for patience and hard work on my part.

Among the activities of the new theatre in that busy New Year of 1931 was the removal of my own private school from South Kensington and its re-erection as the property of the theatre in the famous 'Wells Room' of today. At the same time six young girls were engaged from the school to dance in the opera ballets.

The great thing about the Wells in the early 1930s was that everyone felt so very alerted. Life was filled to the brim with a dedicated sense of purpose and a feeling of modest security, backed by the practical arrangement of a regular but meagre pay packet for everyone. We belonged to both the theatre and the district. We were surrounded by stately old squares and streets of great but neglected beauty; Islington had not yet been 'discovered' as had its distinguished neighbour, Bloomsbury.

Traffic was dominated by the clattering, swaying trams. Their giddy journeys held priority of progress over any of other vehicles bound for the highways of North London. Opposite the Wells' stage door, sunk in a sort of urban garden, were rows of little old Victorian tenement houses. Here the history of the progress of time is grim. By 1939 this spot was found to be 'ideal' for a deep bomb-proof shelter that was hastily and not too well constructed. It received a direct hit right through a ventilation shaft; this resulted in a terrible list of casualties and a removal of the shelter elsewhere. Today, streamlined council flats tower over this piece of land, whose sad history is mercifully lost in time.

Slowly there collected under the roof of the new Sadler's Wells Theatre some of the more interested English dancers. There emerged from the school our own generation of dancers, and it was in the Wells Room that our young school grew ever larger with very young children travelling there to take lessons in the late afternoon after their school hours. One of these was a tiny very talented little girl who had to be moved up a class almost immediately, she is known to us all today as Beryl Grey.

For some of the older students who were used as 'extras' on ballet nights and in the opera ballets the day was a long one, and harder than one would have wished. They were sometimes reminded (as a form of doubtful consolation) of a story in the theatre's past history of the great Grimaldi who ran from Drury Lane to Covent Garden when he had to appear in both theatres on the same night; a hazardous journey that took him across the muddy swamps of the Islington of those days.

From season to season the modest salaries were modestly raised, for it was essential to prove that the ballet could pay its dancers a living wage. Until we could offer a certain financial security, I argued, how could we expect to become a part of the English theatre scene? And what was even more important, how could we expect to have *male* dancers unless we could prove ourselves to be an accepted part of the English theatre, and all that such an achievement would stand for in an immediate foreseeable future? If popular productions took pride of place in those formative years, it was because money just had to come in at the front door so that some of it could get out at the stage door in the artists' pockets.

The guest artists were numerous during the first four years, and a galaxy of stars dazzled Islington, stars that had sprung from the days of the Diaghilev Ballet: Lydia Lopokova, Stanislas Idzikowski, Anton Dolin and last but not least, the young Alicia Markova, once the little girl that I used to help to look after in her very early Diaghilev days. At the Wells we had the privilege to give her an opportunity to study in full *Swan Lake*, *Giselle* and *Casse-Noisette* for the first time in her career. She soon became our first permanent ballerina.

The flurry and the excitement of procuring and mounting the classics! We knew them in England only by hearsay and could only boast of having seen one of them—*The Sleeping Princess* as presented by Diaghilev in 1921 and never given by him again in full.

All our big classical works were mounted under the exacting traditional demands of Serge Nicolai Sergueeff. I was fortunate in persuading him to come to us from Paris, complete with his notation books that contained the Petipa ballets in full, as they were originally notated by Stephanoff. I have a vivid memory of him sitting in a small Paris studio. A lonely little man with his great volumes, patiently and hopefully awaiting a few pupils. He had already paid one visit to England to mount *Giselle* for the Camargo Society at the instigation of Lydia Lopokova. She was very fond of him, 'an honest man; there was never any intrigue on his part', she would repeatedly say. She had known him from her student days at the Maryinsky Theatre as he was the *régisseur* of the Imperial Ballet for some years before the Revolution.

The young Sadler's Wells Ballet had its nights of glamour. Anton Dolin's appearance in *Job* comes to mind, and the ovation given to Markova in her very first *Giselle* (at the Old Vic on one of our exchange visits with the drama company) partnered by Anton Dolin. Lilian Baylis said to me afterwards: 'When he lifted her up, dear, during that curtain call, I found myself crying, clapping and praying to God to find me some more money specially for the ballet. . . .' I have a further memory of Baylis standing on the stage with Gertrude Stein after the première of *The Wedding Bouquet*. Stein and Baylis, a vision not easily erased!

By the middle thirties the younger generation had completely taken over the ballet scene. Their progress up to then had been steady and at times very interesting, but after 1935 it became a force to be reckoned with seriously and entirely on its own. In the first nine years of its life the Islington venture presented works by the following modern English composers: Sir Arthur Bliss, Sir Edward Elgar, Gavin Gordon, Constant Lambert, Sir William Walton and Dr Vaughan Williams. The following great classical ballets were firmly installed in the repertoire: *Casse-Noisette*, *Swan Lake*, *Giselle*, *Coppélia* and *The Sleeping Beauty*.

* * *

Life at the Wells sailed on fair seas until the war years. Then there came a great change in the existence of the young artists, for the Sadler's Wells Theatre was commandeered to provide temporary housing for some of the bombed-out families of Islington. Gone was the quiet security of the 1930s that these young dancers had known in their own theatre. They left their haven and took to the open road for nearly five years. The last wartime production at the Wells was in the summer of 1940. During the time of the fall of France a ballet was produced in Islington aptly, if ironically, named *The Prospect Before Us*.

LILIAN BAYLIS

(The first part was written a few weeks after her death in 1937. Reprinted by kind permission of *The Dancing Times*.)

I take up my pen to endeavour to write about Lilian Baylis. My gratitude towards her is something that I can never fully express. But I would like to give the dancers and dance students of this country some little idea of the work that she has accomplished for the ballet in this country.

For no personal motive had she striven for the last seven years of her life to give the English Ballet a place in the theatre history of this country. It was made clear to Miss Baylis—and made clear at a time when she was harassed financially in every direction—that however successful the projects laid before her might prove to be, the running of such a ballet company would never be a money-making concern. Yet she was the only manager in the country who was prepared to regard such an arrangement as completely satisfactory.

We owe her our greatest debt, for regular employment, artistic achievement and recognition could only be made possible once this selfless point of view was taken by someone who was engaged in the management of a theatre.

So to make this necessary professional start for the English Ballet, the help of one striving already in two other theatrical directions, was asked and given.

31

My first interview with her was in the summer of 1926. That year I wrote two special letters. They contained the outline of a possible scheme for starting an English Ballet in a repertory theatre. I forwarded one to the Old Vic and the other to the Birmingham Repertory Theatre. The Birmingham Theatre turned the project down—but the management of the Old Vic sent for me.

By a curious coincidence Miss Baylis was looking for someone to take charge of her dramatic students' weekly dancing class, and to be responsible for the arrangement of any short dances in the plays. The interview was characteristic. She had my letter in her hand—and said that she thought it showed enthusiasm coupled with a practical mind. She thought I had had enough experience to know my job, and that she liked my face—but had never heard of me professionally. She added that she had been told I was a good dancer—but did not consider that she held any proof, as yet, of my teaching ability, in fact I might be quite hopeless with her drama students. She suggested coming with her producer (Andrew Leigh) to my private studio to see me give my students a lesson. She came—approved and engaged me to do the only work there was to be done at the time. She promised me, that as time went on and things got better, my more ambitious plans would receive her full consideration, and the eventual building of Sadler's Wells would mean the opening of a school in that building, and the nucleus of a ballet installed within its walls.

From here on I have memories of her continual uphill struggle, and a recollection of being dragged along a path that seemed full of insurmountable difficulties. I have a vivid picture of her despair when she was ordered to close the Vic for six months for very necessary repairs. . . . 'The Lord has let me down—I always thought He would see that this theatre was left alone—at least until Sadler's Wells was built.'

I recollect a visit to Sadler's Wells with her, when the theatre was fit to view in its rough state. We stood in the gallery looking down on a vast expanse of white—never again to be viewed

(Left): 'The Traveller'—cartoon of
Ninette de Valois by Nicholas
Legat. (Reproduced by kind
permission of the Legat School of
Ballet)

(Below): Lilian Baylis
'She was in her right environment
at the right moment in history.'

Checkmate: Robert Helpmann and Pamela May. (Photo: Rear Admiral Moore)

Wedding Bouquet: Robert Helpmann and Julia Farron. (Photo: Rear Admiral Moore)

Aurora, pas de deux: Robert Helpmann and Margot Fonteyn. (Photo: Rear Admiral Moore)

Coppélia, Act II: left to right, Elizabeth Kennedy, Elizabeth Miller, Pamela May, Margot Fonteyn, Jill Gregory and Molly Brown. (Photo: Rear Admiral Moore)

(Above): *Casse-Noisette:* left to right, Moyra Fraser, Jean Bedells, Ursula Moreton, June Vincent, (unidentified) and Julia Farron. (Photos: Rear Admiral Moore)

(Below): *Casse-Noisette:* the group includes, Joy Newton, Pamela May, June Brae, Ursula Moreton, Sheila McCarthy, Moyra Fraser, Julia Farron, Robert Helpmann, Michael Somes.

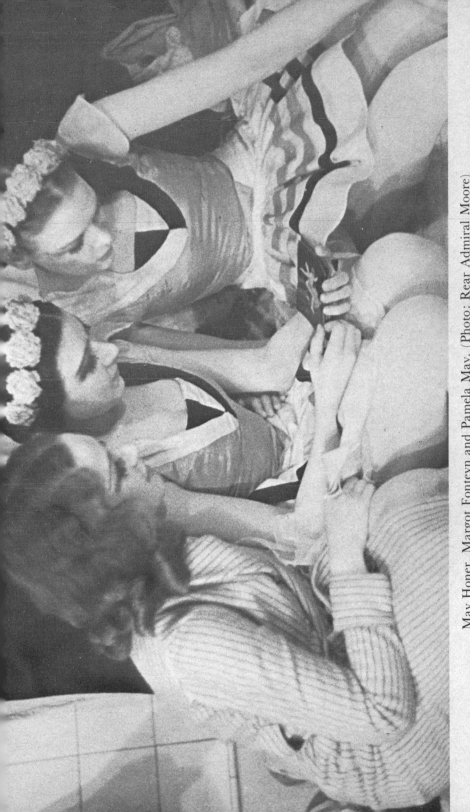

May Honer, Margot Fonteyn and Pamela May. (Photo: Rear Admiral Moore)

Wedding Bouquet: June Brae, Margot Fonteyn and Julia Farron. (Photo: Rear Admiral Moore)

Apparitions: the group includes, Margot Fonteyn, June Brae, Pamela May, Joy Newton, Elizabeth Miller, Gwyneth Mathews, Anne Spicer, Peggy Miller, Robert Helpmann, Leslie Edwards, Alan Carter, Harold Turner and William Chappell. (Photo: Rear Admiral Moore)

(Above): *Job:* Alfred Roderiques (Job), Jean Bedells (Job's wife), and Jack Hart, John Field and Michael Somes as the three messengers. (Photos: E. Mandinian, Reg Wilson)

(Below): revival of *Les Noces*, 1966: Nijinska and Ashton, John Gardner, Edmund Rubbra, Malcolm Williamson, John Lanchbery, Richard Rodney Bennett.

without its cloak of paint, upholstery and seats. She was quiet and preoccupied—and I was struck with the grandeur of the building in its unfinished state, and all that it was going to mean to us in the future.

The rest is common history. Her work for us from 1931 has been one steady aim at stabilising our position. She was sometimes very anxious, and a certain night four years ago showed her in one of those moods that some (who have never understood her) have been inclined to regard as expressions of 'ingratitude'. It was a 'last night' of the season and ballet night at the Old Vic. I was sitting in her office when she came in to join me. We could hear the shouts that greeted the finish of the ballet. 'Hark at them, my dear, shouting away—and you and I have lost £1,000.' I personally felt that I had dropped my £500 over Waterloo Bridge. But that was her genius; her personal staff were always kept within the limits of any feelings of extreme optimism or pessimism. When things were timidly on the mend—fantastic losses were hinted at, for she rightly dreaded any complacency or relaxing of effort. But a really bad financial setback she would take entirely upon her shoulders ... 'never mind, at least everyone is giving of their best—thank God' ... is a remark that I have heard from her so very often. But her gratitude towards those whom she felt had helped to forward her enterprise was unstinting.

Lilian Baylis has given London a permanent ballet company, a theatre, and accommodation for a theatre school.

Her enterprise spells both employment and recognition of the English Ballet. Furthermore, the work has not been thought out just for the present, but for those days, months and years that go to make the future.

In brief, through the courage of one being, there has been planted for you in the middle of London a true heritage. It is your duty to protect this gift—and see that it lives and expands.

I last saw her at the Old Vic two days before she died. Upon that occasion she shared my disappointment over the necessary postponement of *The Sleeping Princess* until the next season. The building must be enlarged before the storing of the innumerable sets and costumes can be undertaken.

At the commencement of each season she has always made a round of the dressing-rooms presenting the artists with a sprig of heather. This autumn, for the first time, she gave everyone rosemary. ...

But she need not have made this change, for it is impossible that the English Ballet could ever forget.

* * *

The early summer of 1974, it is the centenary of the birth of Lilian Baylis. A sudden vision of Southwark Cathedral on Sunday, May the 5th, packed with the old Vic-Wells public from both the North and the South banks. I am with Sir John Gielgud in what seems to be a state of splendid isolation, for we are seated on two very high-backed chairs and severely separated from the rest of the congregation. So stiff and erect, so detached. Do we, I find myself thinking, resemble Henry Moore's 'King and Queen'?

I was exceedingly nervous. I had decided to read lines from a stanza of Wordsworth's poem 'The Perfect Woman', and the first person that I noted sitting in the front row of the congregation was Dame Sybil Thorndike. All I could think of when I rose—as I said to Sir John some months later—was that if I got up and read a poem it was only fair to expect him to get up and dance.

My next memory of that summer is the Old Vic celebration. Here all the Dames of the British Empire who had helped Lilian Baylis in play, opera and ballet productions met together to pay their tribute to her. Cloistered in a typical Old Vic dressing-room we each awaited our separate summons to the stage, which was under the genial but highly professional command of Lord Olivier who marshalled knights and dames alike as the Earl Marshal of theatre pomp and circumstance.

Once more I crossed the river to be present at the planting of a tree outside the Sadler's Wells Theatre and to attend a gala performance of ballet inside the theatre. The little 'Ballet for All' company gave their *Harlequinade* complete with the legendary

34

Grimaldi of Sadler's Wells fame, and the Royal Ballet danced *The Rake's Progress* and *The Wedding Bouquet*, two ballets that were produced during the time of Lilian Baylis' management.

Lastly it was the City Literary Institute, where I spoke with Joan Cross about 'The Lady' to her old public from that part of London.

There were posters all over London that year featuring portraits of 'Centenary Personalities'. Among them were Lilian Baylis and Sir Winston Churchill.

Very different lives; yet I must admit that the words of Sir Winston come into my mind: 'All I can offer you is blood, sweat, toil and tears.' The lady offered the same hospitality to her artists at the Wells.

Lilian Baylis was possessed with the fervour of a Salvation Lass of her period. Her banner took the form of the famous green leaflets that we were asked to 'mislay' in buses and tubes. At one time she marched through the streets of Lambeth and Islington distributing the leaflets at various houses. She would tell the occupants that she had something both beautiful and respectable to give to the general public, and that she had the support and approval of the Lord.

She was in her right environment at the right moment in history: there is always, as we have indeed been told—a time for everything:

> ... And now I see with eye serene
> The very pulse of the machine;
> A breathing thoughtful breath,
> A traveller between life and death;
> The reason firm, the temperate will,
> Endurance, foresight, strength and skill;
> A perfect woman, nobly planned,
> To warn, to comfort and command ...
> *William Wordsworth*

The deep stillness of the Cathedral's vast congregation was the telling answer. ...

EXTRACTS FROM
INVITATION TO THE BALLET

(Published by The Bodley Head in 1937)

A Recollection

One day in 1924, when I was with the Diaghilev Ballet, I was standing as close as I dared behind Massine who was sitting at the piano making notes with his pianist. They were studying the phrasing of a new composition. Suddenly he turned round and said to me: 'Come closer, Ninette, this will be useful to you one day. ...'

ELEMENTARY DANCE STEPS:
(Extract from Chapter 7)

Few appear to realise that the everyday vocabulary of elementary dance steps in the classical school can be found in all the simple steps that comprise the national dances of any country. As an example it is possible to cite the case of the *pas de bourrée*. Because this movement is so frequently executed on the toes, the devotee of the national folk dance would regard it, in composition as well as in execution, as an abnormal, artificial, and completely foreign movement, something the English dancer wishing to promote any national development of the ballet should be averse to using.

This is nonsense. Of course, the development of its correct theatrical execution has brought it to a perfection of artificiality. Yet as explained to the student it is basically no more than 'three transfers of weight from one foot to one foot'. Its complete analysis and, further, its perfection in execution show it to have numerous variations (twenty-three is the usual number acknowledged); these are all known to the technician and are easily recognised in performance, and it is easy to find these variations in many folk dances. It would be possible to arrange a whole *enchaînement* of these variations which would appear as brilliant to witness as they would be intricate to do, but the essence is simple enough and can be discerned many times over in any folk dance.

There are many other steps of equally simple origin that have undergone the same development.

The present cosmopolitan nature of the dance was reached in the eighteenth century, and it is possible to demonstrate that all the suitable dances and movements of the folk dance variety then in existence were collected from various countries; they were then absorbed and their various steps put through a process of very necessary refinement, since they were to form the basis of the classical style which was to become the international idiom of theatrical dancing. But this is not to be confused with the importance of the national dance today, and its relation to the purely native element in a production. It must be remembered that what has been assimilated is of cosmopolitan significance, resulting in an accepted classicism.

ENGLISH REPERTORY BALLET INFLUENCES:
(Extract from Chapter 6)

... The Anna Pavlova Company, founded very shortly after the Diaghilev, is an example of the one company which has existed for any length of time solely as a means of exploiting a single great dancer. In structure the repertoire consisted of nothing of permanent importance. What it presented was the accepted classical ballets, good, bad and indifferent, drastically abridged. This ballet company indulged in every economic concession necessary to enable it to be carried to the four corners of the earth, but the works chosen were only vehicles suitable for the portrayal of the prima ballerina concerned. There is no need to waste time trying to unearth any subtle policy on the part of Anna Pavlova, for the simple reason that this remarkable woman did not have one. She felt the call of the classical tradition as it affected her own bloodstream. Her power, her appeal, and her genius were as personal and as dominating as the sway of Paganini. That her medium was the classical ballet was due to the strategy of destiny rather than the conscious act of Anna Pavlova. She would talk of her efforts towards the safeguarding of the classical ballet, believe in her mission, regard the Diaghilev developments with real consternation, yet do things that many a rigid custodian of classicism found himself unable to accept. If fate had decreed that this artist should be born later, if her genius had developed, for instance, within the four walls of the modern German School, she would have been just as ardent, emphatic and spiritually conservative towards her schooling. But working within the impregnable walls of the classical ballet, she could not shake off its more positive shackles. It was too old, wily and drastic; it demanded its pound of flesh, shone through her and by her, and eventually gained a prestige that even her death could not remove. A method less fundamentally established would have suffered through the passing of this artist, as the work of Isadora Duncan suffered when her life ended.

Yet the Anna Pavlova Company with its great leader and second dancers of no mean skill, its emphasis on the orthodox, and its blatant ballet music of the 'nineties, did not succeed in leaving the dancing world enriched with the galaxy of youthful talent of the classical order that can today be recognised as the fruits of the Diaghilev regime. This despite his wide and varied searchings in every direction of theatrical development, and despite the short-sighted opinion of many that his efforts meant the death of classicism.

Such is the trick of the theatre and its means of remaining master of the situation, Anna Pavlova was turned into the greatest ambassador the classical school has ever known. Diaghilev, who so often worked away from the accepted, died leaving an inheritance of great variety to enrich the classical tradition. It is safe to say that the classical ballet, through the theatre, in one case demanded the custody of individual achievement, and in the other chose to be endowed with a creative movement of importance and far-reaching influence on its subsequent history.

A GREAT BALLET: (Extract from Chapter 2)

Of all the ballets produced during that period, *Les Noces* was most assuredly Diaghilev's greatest achievement. I first heard an orchestral rehearsal, which moved me profoundly, and next attended a rehearsal of the ballet, only to find my interest and understanding receiving further stimulation. To me it is the most spiritually 'Russian' ballet in existence, but complicated to such a degree that a perfect unity of dancers, orchestra, choir and pianos is out of the question unless frequently performed. It is a mass production with no solo work of any great importance, but no one taking part experienced lack of exhilaration on this account; on the contrary, we knew at the time no ballet that gave an artist a more intense emotional interest. One either understands and appreciates from the very first, or else one misses its meaning and qualities altogether. There would be nothing to gain by an argument with any of those critics who, when it was first produced in England, dismissed it as a symptom of Russian neurosis. There is no new movement, in fact nothing to convert anyone to this great work. It is not even an experiment. It arouses a singular state of mind that has no parallel in any other medium. To those who care to understand, it is a rare and isolated instance of combined genius on the part of three people—Stravinsky, Nijinska and Gontcharova. Diaghilev was its sole sponsor, and as such he showed great understanding and courage.*

ENGLISH LYRICAL QUALITY IN CLASSICISM:
(Extract from Chapter 6)

It is strange that England, with no history or tradition of the ballet, possesses at the moment the two most obvious examples of pure classicism.

In Markova there is the mature example, and in Fonteyn the immature. The temperamental and physical qualities displayed by both are such as make them answer to all the demands of the lyrical and romantic requisites of the pure classical ballerina.

We have three brilliant stars of the de Basil Russian Ballet: Toumanova, Baronova and Riabouchinska. Ballets of the *demi-caractère*, modern classicism, or great technical virtuosity, suit them. But in the two English dancers, everything pertaining to their natural talents, temperaments, and appearance, stamp them as the ideal exponents of all roles demanding the cool, crystal-clear requisites of the pure classical performer. This statement need not lead to a controversy on the respective merits of these artists, it is merely a statement of the quality displayed by the executant with regard to her natural tendencies. The distinction is based on division and recognition of type . . . merit need not enter into the discussion. It is sufficient to say that up to the present the three young foreign artists have proved themselves ballerinas of the greater technical powers, while the two English ballerinas have shown the more unusual lyrical qualities associated with pure classicism. I record this to prove that the true classical performer is born

* Frederick Ashton showed the same courage when he had it revived by Nijinska for The Royal Ballet in 1964. This time it was acclaimed by both public and press. *N. de V.*

and not made, for the English dancers have no heritage of schooling comparable with the Russians.

STATUS OF THE ENGLISH REPERTORY THEATRE: (Extract from Chapter 3)

... In England at the moment it is possible to regard the repertory theatre as the offspring as well as the solution of the national or state theatre idea. It is a debatable point among many whether in some ways it may not even prove more satisfactory, for where it presents a slightly more elastic freedom of policy, the state theatre is in continual danger of facing periods of inertia. This condition is brought about by the difficulties of a stringent control through its bureaucratic relations with a government department. *There is on the whole something more democratic and in keeping with this age in the policy of the civic or repertory theatre as sponsored in America and England.*

But the very real advantages of the state-aided theatre are easily explained. It has proved a sure means of founding tradition and harnessing talent, and its continuous employment and pension schemes make the more modest salaries a sound investment for the artist. And in the beginning there is the benefit of the free education and training. The repertory theatre is most certainly responsible for the English ballet, and it is interesting to note that the ballet of today in this country has had very much the same history of adoption as the drama.

The Stage Society sponsored the playwright, producer, and actor, resulting in a Repertory Theatre Movement all over the country and ending in a final doubt as to whether the existence of the Stage Society was any longer necessary; this was assuredly proof of the original courage and organising abilities, for when principles and ideals are universally accepted the world begins to overlook the original source.

This is also the history of the Camargo Ballet* Society, founded by Philip Richardson, Arnold Haskell and Edwin

* Performances were given on a Sunday night and Monday afternoons. *N. de V.*

41

Evans in 1930, helping the Sadler's Wells Theatre Ballet (Vic-Wells) for production on a large scale, and the Mercury Theatre Club for *ballet intime*. The Camargo organised a membership, collected money, and asked the dancers, choreographers, and composers to deliver their efforts, which they did to the best of their untried abilities and under most difficult circumstances.

This new-found freedom of expression gave an opportunity to the expression of crushed and subjected ideas. It was worth all the catastrophes and minor triumphs and, further, the misunderstandings that took up the greater part of the committee meetings.

A few years later the self-same cry that had been raised against the Stage Society was applied to the Camargo Society. The Vic-Wells Ballet was approaching economic security and the company was large enough to take on all the major Camargo productions; so the latter nobly resigned in favour of the repertory company, having done its work more than efficiently for the cause of English ballet.

Thus the ballet came under the protection of the one serious theatre movement in the country, namely, the Repertory. This particular theatre (Sadler's Wells) was in the position, in spite of its struggles, to show a practical way through the utterly hopeless outlook of a few years previously. Here, in a theatre some little distance from the West End of London, could the perfect environment for the development of the ballet become a fact, and the existing dancers of this generation earn a livelihood, in spite of the obvious difficulties and struggles ahead.

Sadler's Wells Theatre is the young dancers' natural environment. Whether, once launched, they remain (as the wise ones do) or whether they seek their fortunes elsewhere, the stamp of such institutions, based on the conception of the artist as a servant of the theatre, remains for ever with them.

They can be true only to that real theatre into which they drifted so gradually that their last day as a student of the theatre and their first day as an artist of the same institution becomes an issue with no real dividing line; for the will and the spell of the place is upon them for ever and a day.

The repertory dancer's debut is not a coming out so much as an evolution.

TOWARDS A NATIONAL THEATRE: (Extract from Chapter 8)

We cannot leave this subject without touching on the question of the rapidly advancing National Theatre Movement in England.

The great move towards a national theatre still continues to progress, and its existence will become an accomplished fact on the day when all the other countries in the world secretly decide that perhaps national theatres are cumbersome institutions and economically embarrassing.

Then will the national theatre of England raise its head majestically on an expensive site in the middle of London.

The writer has, though, in common with so many others, a firm belief in this National Theatre Movement.

It will be anything from fifty to two hundred years behind the erection of most national theatres and consequently untrammelled by those wages of sin which are sometimes simply the heritage of time. It should profit by all the collected mistakes and ruts surrounding such institutions elsewhere. Its offspring are even already illegitimately born and endeavouring to prosper in every corner of the country—they answer to the name of the repertory, the people's, or the civic theatre. These others the national theatre must make its first charge; indeed, it can do no less, for it is they who have done so much to show the necessity for its own very important existence.

A TRIBUTE TO
THE MERCURY THEATRE:
1930–1939

(Written in 1975)

Are these reflections on the beginning of the Establishment to end without any reference to the Mercury Theatre in Notting Hill Gate, where the work of Marie Rambert and Ashley Dukes encouraged the development of the English ballet and the English drama all through the 1930s?

'The Ballet Club' was the foundation of today's Ballet Rambert, and the home of certain artists who did much to forward the general cause when Sadler's Wells was able, by 1933, to offer a number of them a livelihood and further development of their talents in a larger theatre.

Not that their work in Islington ever interfered with the valuable work in progress in their own small theatre. They continued to appear at the Mercury in the weekend performances and on their free nights from the Wells. They continued under the above arrangement right up to the war.

It proved itself beneficial to both theatres. However good the dancers and however interesting the work, the Mercury was too small to provide proper salaries for these artists. But professional work for a number of the Mercury dancers could actually be obtained outside the conventional commercial theatre,

44

in an environment dedicated to the progress of English ballet, which enabled them to continue to uphold the work and the ideals of their own theatre. And the benefit to the Wells? This constituted the speeding up of that search for the very necessary talent from outside that was important to link up with our own numbers at the beginning. The aims and the training of the Mercury dancers were the aims and training that we were looking for, and in preference to the average run of the commercial theatre's professional dancers.

As the 1930s moved on a two-way flow developed. Old Mercury programmes will show the appearance of the young Margot Fonteyn, June Brae and others from the Wells in the weekend performances at Notting Hill Gate. Ashton continued up to the war to choreograph for Rambert as well as on his increasing scale at the Wells. Both ventures joined forces for the Camargo Society productions.

Everybody loved the Mercury Theatre. In spite of its smallness, its atmosphere for me was not far removed from that of the Festival Theatre, Cambridge, and the Abbey Theatre, Dublin. There was dedication; there was the love of the development of the theatre for itself; there was always a stream of dancers, actors and actresses ready to offer their services.

On the part of Dame Marie Rambert there was a devoted service given to the young artists that came her way, and Ashley Dukes—a distinguished author and critic—saw that his little theatre served the young actors, actresses and dramatists of the day.

The work was executed on a miniature and very economical scale. Perfection was aimed at and often achieved in its various activities. Here was first seen a ballet that is still a major item in the more contemporary Ballet Rambert Company of today—Antony Tudor's moving *Dark Elegies*. At the beginning of the war there was staged, in a not very much larger theatre, Andrée Howard's one act gem—*Fête Étrange*. This is now in the repertoire of the Royal Ballet.

I think I loved such theatres and their efforts perhaps as

45

much as I loved developing and giving security to those who came my way from such places, and continued to serve the place they came from whenever possible. The Abbeys, the Festivals, the Old Vics, the Wells', and the Mercurys were beacons that had to be kept alight, and their efforts rewarded by the fight to forward the movement of the repertory theatre, so that the widespread possibilities at last became a fact—with results that can be seen sweeping through the country today.

This little note of gratitude to the Mercury Theatre closes on one further comment. Frederick Ashton, the 'Petipa' of the English ballet did not come from Marseilles, but from Notting Hill Gate.

PHASE II

The 1940s and the 1950s

The 1940s and the 1950s

Years of gloom followed by a flood of light. Through the dark ages of the war to the renaissance of peace danced the Islington establishment. Paradoxically, it was the war years that worked in favour of the Sadler's Wells Ballet's future security. Our steady progress at the Wells was cut short in the summer of 1940, but only in the end to increase our audiences in every city and town of England that was our wartime duty to visit for the next five years.

In the middle of the 1940s I found myself requested to move the little establishment from Sadler's Wells to the new big establishment planned for the Royal Opera House, Covent Garden.

By February 1946, the Royal Opera House had discarded its wartime role of a dance hall and was ready to receive the Sadler's Wells Ballet. We opened the Opera House and kept it open until we were joined by the newly-formed Opera Company—about nine months later. A second, smaller company was formed for the Sadler's Wells Theatre.

The years that followed were filled with rapid growth, and many artists and ballets became famous.

1. The ballet school became a residential co-educational school at White Lodge, Richmond Park, with Arnold Haskell as its first director and Ursula Moreton as ballet principal.

49

2. New York was frequently visited by the company, and wide tours of the States were made.
3. I submitted a memorandum to the Covent Garden board of directors concerning the future status and the necessity of a change of name.
4. We received a Royal Charter and became the Royal Ballet and the Royal Ballet School. The Charter covered both the big and little company.*
5. We established the Turkish National Ballet and the Persian National Ballet.

In this section are writings relevant to the time, whether written today or during the actual period itself.

* In the year 1946 the smaller company returned to the Sadler's Wells Theatre, its original home. It is now known as the Sadler's Wells Royal Ballet under the direction of Peter Wright.

N. de V.

FIVE ARCHITECTS OF THE BALLET

CONSTANT LAMBERT

He has been much written about through the years; and I have expressed my appreciation of him many times—in print and on the radio. Yet here and now, just twenty-five years after his death, there is need for a song of praise to be sung for this important 'architect' of our war years.

Constant Lambert held himself responsible, and at a grim time in our history, for the musical standards of our wartime productions, and the same vigilance was also bestowed on the standard of the playing.

There was never any question of the war requiring his services for more militant purposes; his lameness, due to an accident as a boy, debarred him from any form of military service. I mention this because he was consequently regarded as a very valuable member of the musical world in general, hard pressed as they were at such a time.

Yet by the end of the first year of the war (with Sadler's Wells Ballet short of its orchestra, and many of its most valuable scores lost in the invasion of Holland) Constant Lambert was still to be found with us, in the pit as one of our two pianists; his approach to this work was meticulous, the playing had to be first rate; this was his aim, and he saw that it was fulfilled.

After another grim year had passed we were in a position to reinstate an orchestra. The theatre in general, with what it could offer as a solace to a war-riddled country, was winning through; and the Sadler's Wells Ballet was increasing its popularity throughout the country.

It is the morning of our first 1942 wartime orchestral rehearsal. I can still hear and see his brisk attack on a rather veteran orchestra rehearsing *The Sleeping Beauty*. There is nothing more heartening or more exhilarating than a true professional demanding *his* money or your life, and this was the very thing that Constant was asking of his players through the medium of a Tchaikovsky score—a score that would be heard up and down the country for some years as a part of our wartime signature tune.

In an interval on that memorable morning I found him chuckling to himself, made happy by the lively remark of an old member of the Sadler's Wells Orchestra: 'Tchaikovsky comes up nice and fresh, don't he, Sir?' Constant was delighted.

When new ballets had to be mounted, thick with wartime restrictions, Lambert was faced with many orchestral compromises, score reductions and difficult rehearsal schedules. Yet still came the demand for perfection, and the compromises were always handled skilfully. It was the echo of this frontal attack from the orchestra pit that became such a challenge on the stage. Somehow it compelled us to cope with the monthly sapping of our strength by the devastating military call-up.

A new shape emerges; it is February 1946. I have the memory of the same baton at work; the same energy bestowed on the same ballet score; but this time it is at the first rehearsal within the plush surround of the Royal Opera House, Covent Garden.

Yes; it had indeed come up again all 'nice and fresh' and within a scene of splendour that was far removed from our recent turbulent yesterdays.

It is for me an unfading picture; the great Opera House, discarding its mad dance-hall atmosphere of the war years, to return to sounds from its orchestra pit of the soaring melodies of a famous ballet score; a scene that warmed the hearts of us all as we awaited the emergence of our young male dancers from the forces.

There was more than melody in that famous pit; there was an equally famous 'beat' that, as it had in the past, would again in the future alert both players and dancers and continue to demand the best from them—and nothing less than the best.

It was a morning that witnessed the Sadler's Wells Ballet's musical awakening in full, and through the vision of one of the company's finest architects.

*　　*　　*

The above is a sketch written to fit in with a certain period in the development of today's Royal Ballet, and the part that Constant Lambert and others played in it.

How am I to see him in retrospect as a friend, an adviser, and a man of intellect and personality in our midst?

He was, as many a brilliant mind, distinctly volatile. At one moment you argued with an intelligent wayward 'bluecoat' boy; at another with an old head on young shoulders showing a depth of knowledge that left you blushing over your own shortcomings; another time he would be outrageous and not over-respectful of any elder or better, then you were confronted with an attack of acute conservatism, ridiculing his own avant-garde. He could be humorous about donnish musical minds, placing Sir Henry Wood on a pedestal above them all, and upholding the professional common sense of the Edwin Evanses of this world in comparison with some of the views expressed by the critics of the weekly papers, and as a further diversion I can recall a hilarious account of the acute discomfort that he had suffered when he found himself sitting through *The Ring* at Strasbourg. . . .

Down through the years he wore his many-coloured coat, always hating any atmosphere of self-conscious intellectuality, and when such moments occurred this particular intellectual adopted a form of bucolic opposition. In spite of his fluctuating temperament, I maintain that Lambert's inborn common sense and knowledge of true values were always apparent.

If temporarily irritated by the ballet classics, he would express his boredom with Tchaikovsky, and then go into the orchestra pit to conduct one of the composer's ballets as no one else has done since.

When he had had too many drinks he was either exasperating, gloomy or very funny. One evening in New York after a good but somewhat taut performance of *Le Lac des Cygnes*, he made the following cryptic remark: 'When the *pas de trois* came on and turned out to be *pas de six* I knew things were getting out of hand.'

He was observant, and possessed a shrewd judgement of his friends and acquaintances. Then there would be a complete somersault when his ingrained superstitious mind took over, and we had to accept anything from visions worthy of extreme Celtic twilight to poltergeist experience beyond my down-to-earth mentality.

I do not want the real Constant Lambert to get out of perspective. He had in him a strain of extraordinary logical reasoning powers, and if he had any interest or belief in the people that he was working with, they could only become even more aware of the great qualities that he was displaying. Thus for years I watched a turbulent sea that had an undercurrent of smooth waters, a gulf stream that could help balance the temperature with a sympathetic understanding of the rise and fall of thinking, planning and doing.

Musically speaking he had his prejudices, for most musicians feel strongly about the use of certain composers for ballets. He always said that he would never conduct a ballet mounted to any music of Mozart, nor would he encourage the use of symphonies. He did not really want Ashton to produce *Symphonic Variations*, and he was no real admirer of Vaughan Williams' score for *Job*. Yet such was his respect for true professionalism that he attacked with interest the re-scoring of *Job* for a small orchestra at Vaughan Williams' request. It was brilliantly executed.

He loved musical dancers, but showed no shock or sorrow if he discovered that this did not necessarily lead to any real musical appreciation on their part. 'Tell that man to stop asking me about Beethoven's symphonies and just try to keep *time*'— was the exasperated remark shot at me one day.

Orchestral players adored him; his deft leadership and lack of pomposity went straight to the heart of even the most seasoned members of the orchestra.

He was at his best when seated with us at the piano working out cuts, sequences, and the general development of a piano score that he was arranging. Long silences with a foot tapping, a hand conducting, a muffled hum through the cigarette with its endless fall of ash; there would be a sudden lean forward on to the score, and the appearance of several clear firm notation marks; once more the straightened position and the one-man band restarted.

He had a carefully acquired knowledge of different types of dancers; an awareness, through his powers of observation, of weakness and strength in the all-over picture of technical prowess, and sympathetic understanding shown where licence could be permitted that was not to the detriment of the musical or choreographic flow. Yet he was a great disciplinarian, and generally insisted on discussing tempo with the choreographer concerned, or in the case of the classical revivals, with me. His word was law, and a law respected by all the artists ... 'When Constant makes a tempo change it doesn't worry us, he always makes you want to respond' ... in other words, he always knew when they could respond to his demands. The present liberties taken (and I will cite the second act of *Le Lac des Cygnes* as danced by any company) would not have been tolerated. Leisurely elongation, however skilful, would have received no response to its telepathic communication of 'Stop the music, I don't want to go on'—the performer would have found himself panting along behind a stream of missed bars.

Yet he loved and appreciated a good virtuoso just as he did a good melody.

It was never quite clear to me what his position was with the musical hierarchy. In those days they 'placed' people, and the younger school awaited the result of their placing. Constant was no 'yes' man; those of the older school that upheld him and admired him were his special and very noticeable champions, while I have always felt that there were others who regarded him with caution; they were partly bewildered, and did not want to pass too hasty a judgement on someone with such a medley of gifts.

As a composer I would say that he was not capable of anything less than good and interesting work, but for health reasons in the end this side never really fulfilled its original expectations, in spite of the fact that he was the first English composer to write a ballet for Diaghilev.

He was the greatest ballet conductor and adviser that this country has had, and the musical world has labelled him as such. Towards the end this was for him a very real frustration. I know through conversations with him how much he would have liked to have had far more musical interests outside ballet; he felt, and not without reason, that he was a victim of type casting.

We, the ballet world, devoured him and drained him of everything that he had to give us from 1931 to within two years of his death. For a brief period at the end he was only a guest artist. But he had allowed things to slip too far in the last few years of his life to make anything in the form of a completely fresh outlook possible. His health was not up to such an effort, in fact it could only just sustain what he had already achieved. This tragic situation did not help his genuine wish to break fresh ground and leave the ballet world that he had served with so much love and enthusiasm.

Even today he is irreplaceable in the ballet: there is no one to equal him in that all-round knowlege and intellectual understanding demanded of this eclectic side of the theatre world.

He laid a foundation stone for us from which things could continue to spring, and here it can be seen in retrospect that he had all along shown second sight.

His last ballet, *Tiresias*—produced a short time before his death—had a very bad reception. One of those hysterical attacks that, in the end, if he had lived and the ballet with him, the work would probably have been reassessed, for there were too many fine moments in the ballet to condemn it out of hand.

'Three Blind Mice' ran the heading of one *review*—I read on, and discovered that the three were Lambert, Ashton and myself.

When I am struck blind again may it be in such equally worthy company.

FREDERICK ASHTON

(Published in *The Dancing Times*, London, 1942.
Addition 1974)

Frederick Ashton has been with the Sadler's Wells Ballet as dancer and principal choreographer since the 1935–36 season. He joined the company just as Markova left, and his influence on the development and success of the Ballet since that time cannot be too strongly stressed. Averaging three productions per season, this credits him with about eighteen ballets in the last six years.

His career at the Wells may be divided into two parts: his contribution to the repertoire and his influence on the dancers.

With the exception of *The Sleeping Princess*, not produced until 1939, Sadler's Wells had, for eighteen months prior to his entry, mainly concentrated on reviving the big classical ballets: *Giselle, Casse-Noisette, Coppélia,* and *Le Lac des Cygnes* were produced in quick succession. When Ashton came it can be said that the independent development, choreographically, of Sadler's Wells Ballet really began.

His task was a formidable one, his company of dancers youthful and, with the exception of Helpmann and Turner, not very experienced. Further, the theatre's resources were financially anything but unlimited.

During the season 1935–36 he produced *Baiser de la Fée*, *Les Patineurs*, *Nocturne* and *Apparitions*. It can be said that in six months these four works placed the Sadler's Wells Ballet within reach of the goal that it had been striving after for four years. Had he failed he might have smashed us. As it turned out, he succeeded—and played a major role in the making of us.

That this English choreographer succeeded in establishing himself, when given his first opportunity in a big theatre harbouring a regular company, is due to an important factor. He has a remarkable sympathy with, and understanding of, any artist's particular individuality. He 'presents' his young dancers in such a way that the balance between the whole and the part is fused with a skill that amounts to genius.

I would like to take the opportunity of stressing this particular gift for the benefit of the many young choreographers in the country. The war is giving them many opportunities that the older generation of English choreographers (in the piping days of peace with competition and general theatrical enterprise on a large scale) never experienced. Let all of us study Ashton's work from this angle—his complete sense of proportion between role and artist. The issue is never forced, nor is the artist exploited, yet he always avoids a completely mechanical acceptance of his creation. He has (and here I speak as director of a ballet company) the ideal psychological approach towards the dancer. The executant has only to listen and to discipline himself within reason to realise that he is in hands where knowledge and understanding form that rarity—a harmonious partnership.

As a gift, I cannot say that this highlight in Ashton's approach to his work is to be noted among the younger choreographers over here at the moment. I think they must realise that their own inexperience as artists of the theatre and the tendency towards extravagant praise from the critics makes their case a difficult one. So I would remind them of the wealth of work Ashton has left for them to view from time to time.

The war has temporarily taken Ashton from us. I can only prattle of what he has achieved for us. It is an added sadness for me that the gradual draining of male dancers from the Sadler's Wells Ballet is making it increasingly difficult to maintain many of his major works in the repertory.

He has, in spite of offers from abroad, stuck to the English Ballet at home throughout the early part of the war. I have the proud memory, twenty-four hours before the invasion of Holland, of seeing an entire Dutch audience rise to its feet as it applauded *Dante Sonata*. This gesture made by a foreign country towards an English company and an English choreographer was utterly sincere and spontaneous, and I will leave you to dwell on its significance.

*   *   *

History has written the rest for me; for this artist went from strength to strength once he was able to return to his root in the theatre world.

There is one aspect of Ashton's career that is unique to him among his contemporary choreographers in this country.

He had just fulfilled six years of consecutive work with the then Sadler's Wells Ballet when the war intervened, cutting him off at the most important moment of his development.

During the next four years he knew what it was to be suspended in time. It was possible for writers and painters to experience brief moments of self-expression in spite of their war duties, but such temporary respite was not possible for a choreographer. Ashton accepted quietly the setback contributed by the general upheaval that left few untouched. Occasionally he would be able to pay us a fleeting visit, and was always sympathetic and encouraging over my efforts not to let things slip too far. Towards the end of the war he did get two months' respite to mount a ballet for us—*The Quest*—with music by Sir William Walton and scenery and costumes by John Piper.

59

Ashton's re-establishment of himself once we were settled at Covent Garden in the early winter of 1946 was remarkable, if, understandably, it was at first spasmodic, for sensibility and thought had known procrastination, and the power of action had to be resolved now freedom was once more to be his experience. His first real comeback was *Symphonic Variations*; this ballet was actually staged in the late spring of 1946. There then followed a period when the talent and the inspiration flowed— but unevenly.

What was the result when this equilibrium was restored? Swiftly there comes to mind *Scenes de Ballet, Cinderella, La Fille Mal Gardée, The Two Pigeons, Enigma Variations, The Dream, Homage to the Queen*, to mention but a few from a series of outstanding works. From the Islington days we had revivals in the form of *Façade, Les Rendezvous*, and *A Wedding Bouquet*.

But the choreographic achievement of Ashton is not for me to write about; I will leave it to those who can be more objective, who can give the accurate breakdown that it has earned, without regard for personal preferences.

You cannot watch an artist through the more tentative approach of his early years to complete fulfilment at a later date, without indulging in your own special enjoyment of his efforts.

The Ashton scene is kaleidoscopic. I do not search among the dignified accepted classics of his that have received the accolade of the entire world of ballet. I search for my own special loves.

It is like going through a crowded bookcase; you take out certain books to read again and again, not because you are frightened of forgetting their contents, only because you cannot forget them and do not want to forget them.

I first speak to you of *Birthday Offering*, choreographed for the celebration of our twenty-fifth year. Here, in this ballet, was an example of what I spoke of in the first part of this article written thirty-four years ago. By the middle 1950s his approach bore the mark of the passage of years. He was no longer working on promising young artists, but on ballerinas of today's Royal Ballet.

What did Ashton highlight for them with that delicate instinctive touch of his? Let us recall some of the dances arranged for certain ballerinas in this ballet.

In a darting crisp variation for Rowena Jackson he caught her speed; the dance gave an impression of a swift in flight. Svetlana Beriosova was a picture of serene nobility, her Slav birthright left to express itself, uninhibited by alien mannerisms that could have been imposed on it by the choreography. Nadia Nerina, with her immense gift of soft-flowing but strong elevation, swept the stage in a series of beautifully designed movements that overnight became her unchallenged heritage, while Beryl Grey's always unruffled and unhurried technical facility was presented with ingenuity.

Fonteyn came as a climax. Here was majesty expressed delicately with movements that mirrored her inborn elegance. This particular dance was one of those imaginative understatements that Ashton so often asked of her.

To say that he had them all taped gives a crude but accurate enough description of his subtle yet harmonious control of their different styles, highlights and personalities.

I can still see *Ondine* as the company danced the work on the opening night at the Kirov Theatre in Leningrad. It was the performance that led to Mr Kruschev's remark: 'Look at those girls, they might all be Russians!'

This was a very great ballet composed to fine music; but like anything really good it needed to be seen many times before the full impact of both its artistry and craftsmanship could be fully experienced. It was a skilful example of the Ashton sense of theme and image development. It was a ballet where the music and choreography just had to form a true sense of partnership.

The public looked on it as a vehicle for Fonteyn, for she undoubtedly gave, in this instance, her finest performance of a modern ballet. I feel, though, that the role symbolised, subcons-

61

ciously on Ashton's part, a dedication to Pavlova. Fonteyn seemed to become his inspired tool, and he appeared to reincarnate the spirit of Pavlova in the role itself, and infused Fonteyn with the message. Again, he understood how her discipline, her artistry and her pliability would not fail to absorb the choreography that nevertheless, for the writer, aroused the memory of a very different personality.

I feel that *Ondine* contained the greatest account of his ensemble work. It is perhaps the one example where an Ashton ballet subjects itself to the force of its ensembles. Three of them were pure choreographic gems; the 'water nymph's dance' in Act I, where water was symbolically portrayed through the multiple vision of every form of swiftly undulating movement— cascade, fountain, rapid stream and waterfall; it was all there in a medley of choreographic flow.

The *divertissement* in the last act was a work of originality and astuteness. I do not know any ensemble that found me so riveted and filled with excitement at every performance; it formed a rare partnership with its very distinguished and unusual musical accompaniment. It was also outstandingly right for the disciplined approach of an English *corps de ballet*.

On the whole my joy was rather solitary. This ensemble never received the accolade that it deserved.

The third great moment was a study in craftsmanship. It showed an orderly sense of disposition, resulting in the achievement of an economical example of a vivid theatrical sense. I am referring to the shipwreck scene; it evolved itself into a spectacular piece of romanticism that, in its detail work, suggested at times the frenzy to be found in a Delacroix painting.

Out of the past, certain highlights intrude on my memory. The solos of the seasons in *Cinderella*, the dance of the stars in the same ballet, the ballroom scene in *Apparitions*, the final scene in *Nocturne*, and some skilful additional numbers wrought in the Petipa ballets.

I will stop there; it is not my idea to force my memory, but to recall what returns to my mind with the ease of a recognition that leaves the original impact unchanged by the passage of nearly fifty years.

All through the first part of Ashton's career with the Royal Ballet—*née* Sadler's Wells—there were two great influences at work on him, Constant Lambert and Sophie Fedorovitch. Fonteyn proved to be his muse from 1935. But he served all the artists of the company loyally and brought out the material that the Establishment had dedicated itself to prepare for him and others.

Often in our many private conversations we would discuss influences. We always came back to our joint love and admiration of Pavlova. He saw her dance first when he was a young boy in South America, I saw her when I was a young teenager in London. (Wednesday afternoons in the summer found me in the upper circle of the Palace Theatre. Here I wrote copious notes recording *The Dying Swan*—with the musical phrasing carefully noted—as she danced it at that time.)

Our reminiscences always finished with a mutual observation: 'There has never been anything like her.'

All my life I have remembered her intrinsic head movements, and in Ashton's choreography there is often to be seen that electrifying and magnetic flow of movement that belonged to the Pavlova he saw in South America.

Ashton can be regarded as the English choreographer who responded from the beginning to the lyrical quality that smooths out the delicate precision to be found in our English classical dancers. His choreography has the same fundamental approach. Throughout his career there has been this true partnership, where sympathy and understanding have been equally divided.

ROBERT HELPMANN

(This article first appeared as the introduction to *Robert Helpmann: Studies by Gordon Anthony*, published by Home and Van Thal, London, 1946.)

The Sadler's Wells School has seen many young artists pass through its classrooms to the company. The first impressions made by most of these dancers I must confess to have forgotten. But there are two figures I recollect with unusual clarity of vision. I can still visualise Margot Fonteyn, the part of the room she occupied, and the exercise she was doing when I entered the children's class one morning during her first week in the school.

I remember next Robert Helpmann. Wrapped in a large overcoat, he entered the Wells room in the middle of a class, and I felt that something quite important had happened. The entrance was discreet and well-timed: I thought—personality. He was polite but quite self-assured, so, I decided, unselfconscious; an odd resemblance to Leslie Henson made me hope for humour, and a thoughtfulness about the face in repose was reminiscent of Massine. This unknown young man impressed me with a strange sense of power; here, possibly, was an artist of infinite range ...

During the subsequent conversation I realised that 'Robert Helpmann' was the boy the distinguished actress Margaret Rawlings had written to me about from Australia. Her note had been full of enthusiasm for his undeveloped talent. Following the interview he was taken into the school, and after a week's work, my log-book was completed as follows:

On the credit side—talented, intelligent, great vitality and humour, cute as a monkey, quick as a squirrel; a sense of the theatre and his own possible achievements therein.

On the debit side—academically backward, technically weak,

64

Constant Lambert
'He laid a foundation stone for us
from which things could continue
to spring ... he had all along
shown second sight.'

Frederick Ashton
1942, the year of his call-up to the
R.A.F. 'He has the ideal
psychological approach towards a
dancer.' (Photo: Cecil Beaton)

Robert Helpmann
With Margot Fonteyn and Celia
Franca in *Hamlet*. 'Downright
professionalism ... not by chance,
but by studied application.' (Photo:
Tunbridge-Sedgwick)

Margot Fonteyn
'As musical as she is unified in her
approach to movement.'
(Photo: Lenare)

Sophie Fedorovitch (left) with the
famous teacher, Vera Volkova. 'She
was never known to permit a line
or curve of her design to interfere
with or confuse the clarity of the
choreography.' (Photo: G. B.
Wilson)

(Above): Ninette de Valois
Sculpted in her year of retirement,
1963, by F. E. McWilliam. (Photo:
Donald Southern)

(Left): Ninette de Valois
Taken in 1946, at the time of the reopening
of the Royal Opera House. (Photo:
Angus McBean)

The Royal Opera House

(Above): a wartime photograph when it was being used as a dance hall.

(Below): a ballet Gala performance in 1960 in honour of General and Madame de Gaulle.

lacking in concentration, too fond of a good time, too busy having a good time.

Summary—he was to enter the company at once and to work his way up from the corps de ballet, combining this work with strict routine study in the school.

By a series of leaps and bounds he set about making short work of my curriculum. The leaps were by no means faultless academically, and the bounds may sometimes have been ahead of time through lack of serious competition; but no matter, here was a newcomer among us destined to play a great part in the youthful English ballet.

At the end of six months he received his first big chance— Satan in *Job*. He danced the role in the autumn of 1933 as successor to Anton Dolin—a great ordeal for this young dancer; but he was young enough to attribute the whole ordeal to the fact that he was following Dolin; I do not think that the custody of an important role in itself worried him. The two performances were worlds apart in conception and realisation. Dolin had carried *Job* through brilliantly in the early Camargo performances as a *tour de force*—physically he was the perfect replica of the Blake drawings; Helpmann caught the spirit of Blake, and the true outline, both plastically and musically. I quote with pleasure and agreement Richard Capell's remark ... 'There is a wild poetry about his dancing. . . .'

His next opportunity? A small one, but astutely taken. It was Hilarion in our first production of *Giselle*, with Markova's debut in the name part, and Dolin's guest performance as Albrecht. Sufficient to say that *The Times* considered that he should be watched (an idea obviously shared by the new Hilarion); whenever on the scene, however distinguished the company, he held his own and collected his public from stalls to gallery. Lilian Baylis had begun to pick him out. 'I like the boy, dear, who puts too much brilliantine on his hair; do stop him, his head's rather large anyway, and it makes one keep looking at him.' 'Perhaps,' I suggested, 'that is what he means you to do, perhaps he thinks the brilliantine just another good idea. . . .'

The spring of 1934 saw the first role created for him—the Master of Treginnis in Geoffrey Toye's ballet, *The Haunted Ballroom*. In this his considerable dramatic scope was evident. The next year was devoted to the study of the classics. Sergueeff mounted *Le Lac des Cygnes* in its entirety for the first time, with Helpmann and Markova, and the former had already taken over from Dolin and Judson in *Giselle*. In all three roles his mimetic gifts stood comparison with any previous artist's performance, and regular academic work and experience was steadying the young artist's background. Helpmann had become a dancer of the first rank in the younger school, comparable indeed with any foreign contemporary.

Further and greater opportunities occurred from the autumn of 1935 onwards. Frederick Ashton had joined the company as permanent choreographer. During the next few years *Nocturne, Apparitions, Dante Sonata* and *A Wedding Bouquet*, to mention four new works, had their leading male roles sustained by Helpmann. But during this period he succeeded in serving two masters equally loyally and well. He met with considerable success in many of my ballets—notably as the Red King in *Checkmate*, and he succeeded Walter Gore in *The Rake's Progress*. In *The Prospect Before Us* I created in Mr O'Reilly a role that was deliberately inspired by Helpmann. He has made of this fantastic Rowlandson figure an endearing and entrancing character study of a balletic clown—culminating in the now famous inebriated dance that will have to be buried with its first performer.

Helpmann is not a choreographer in the purest sense of the word. He is not concerned with choreography for choreography's sake. He has nothing to give outside his own powers of observation and comment on some literary or psychological theme. He says all in direct terms of the theatre, a theatre seen fearlessly and aggressively through the eyes of a young man of the twentieth century. He has no use for his own carefully studied tradition of the ballet or the demands of the true balletomane. All spells vitality harnessed to controversy— yet he cannot help showing his knowledge of the very tradition that he has temporarily discarded. He fuses and drives home his production with a severe theatrical discipline and when all is completed the work emerges as a creation with a very nationalistic stamp.

The sum of Helpmann's brief period of choreography has been to bestow on the English theatre in general a gift from one of its specialised branches—the Ballet. *Hamlet*, the ballet to the music of Tchaikovsky, is an example of a masterly control of most of the crafts of the theatre. Lewis Casson stated to me that its influence might well be 'felt in every future production of *Hamlet*, the play'. It was the *drama* world of the theatre that upheld the importance of this dramatic ballet. The ballet world remained in the rear to bestow a guarded opinion, or to show open hostility. Their attitude was not necessarily churlish, allowing for their orthodox requisites and standards, but their judgement was at fault if they imagined that, by failing to qualify as a *ballet* in their narrow sense of the word, this work was not contributing anything to our honour in the theatre generally. *Miracle in the Gorbals* again adapts this positive form. This work shook the Parisian public to the core. 'The English Ballet has taught me something new,' was Boris Kochno's brief comment when he met me a few minutes after the fall of the curtain.

We have in this artist one of those peculiar forces that occasionally enters the realm of the theatre at certain intervals as a stimulus. We cannot explain, but we may not ignore. Robert Helpmann is perhaps a greater force behind the vitality of the English ballet than we care to realise. He defies the laws of gravity, not as Nijinsky did, but as he likes to do ... the legendary giant in his seven-league boots, striding from ballet to film, ballet to play—but always back to the ballet.

Exasperating sometimes—snatching at his many theatrical irons, all in the fire and all red-hot. But the ultimate approach is always thorough, the effort sincere. Neither is he a theatrical snob. I have seen him on tour rush from the last act of a full-length classical ballet to get to the second house of the local music-hall. For what? To worship at the shrine of some skilful music-hall comedian. ... He will return, looking and feeling as if all that matters is to give such a performance as he has just witnessed—and I begin to suspect that the ballet may have robbed the music-halls of another Grock, an Australian one.

One's affection and esteem is increased by his downright professionalism—which is his, not by chance, but by studied application.

So let us accept his stardom, for his fame has not been achieved without practical self-sacrifice. He has worked devotedly, intelligently, and remarkably rationally for anyone with such wide and varied theatre interests. Today he is the victim of balletomane mass-hysteria. Will he survive it? I think so, for he stands every chance with such a fortunate background. He reached his height in the ballet world as a permanent member of a conservative institution. He has also his rational, though freedom-loving, colonial background. Born a son of *Aries*, he is affiliated to the pioneer sign, and as a native of Australia he springs from an ancestry of pioneers.

MARGOT FONTEYN

(Introduction written to *Studies of Margot Fonteyn*
by Gordon Anthony. Phoenix House Ltd. 1951.
British Books Centre Inc. New York)

Margot Fonteyn has followed in the footsteps of Markova, and England has thus produced two ballerinas of international fame in the last sixteen years. When Markova left Sadler's Wells in 1935, Margot Fonteyn, then a gifted child of sixteen, stepped from the ranks of the *corps de ballet* to fulfil her destiny. For such a young dancer her mode of development for the first four years was ideal; the ballet appeared only twice every week at the Sadler's Wells Theatre, from the end of September to the beginning of May. In between seasons it toured for seven weeks; the rest of the summer was devoted to a long vacation.

The war set us many difficult conditions to contend with during the ensuing years. Fonteyn's gifts were unavoidably exploited and her stamina from time to time put to a severe test. Life was uncomfortable; the lack of sleep during the various air-raid periods, the curtailment of many foodstuffs essential to an athlete's diet, and the ceaseless performances all over the country gave one anxiety about the possible effect of such conditions on her progress towards perfection. But she always showed fortitude and sense of proportion beyond her years, and thus emerged, at the end of her experiences, a rare and exquisite ballerina—known to and loved by a multitude of people throughout the country.

She was the Sleeping Beauty whose role in real life was reversed—she was to awaken London's golden Opera House from its long sleep, a sleep which had lasted through the grimmest sequence of nights that it had known. But our Sleeping Beauty herself awoke to find that overnight she also, like other great dancers before her, could claim to be without a rival. As she stepped on to the stage that night in February, 1946, she was not a stage princess celebrating her birthday but a great dancer celebrating her birthright. It had taken English ballet just fifteen years to prove its worth. Fonteyn, who had never wavered in her integrity, her hard work, and her loyalty towards the institution that can proudly claim to have made her, was there to lead her companions to triumph.

Fonteyn now bears an international name and makes individual guest performances in other countries, apart from her official appearances with the English ballet. As Fonteyn's early teacher and adviser, and as her present director and sometimes teacher, what have I to say? Very little; the conventional has been said so many times, and what is not conventional is subtle and intangible. We have here an artist whose greatness is the result of the impact of some inner force on her art; therefore we are not only confronted with Fonteyn, the exquisite machine in motion, but with Fonteyn, the spiritual force behind the machine.

This ballerina is a great artist by design and a great star by accident. It is well to remember that many a celebrity answers to this description in reverse. The artist develops from within and the star assimilates from without. The impact of life, impressions, and the highly developed ego are the ingredients that produce the latter; the forces that are at work in the former do not use such tangible experiences. The sources are spiritual, intangible; we accept the result without demanding the usual concrete evidence.

This is Fonteyn's power; we accept her unconditionally. She never confronts us with nor appears to be interested in the more obvious. She is concerned with what she feels is true, and the expected or unexpected as a form of ornamentation is alien to her approach. We say that truth is beauty, and it seems that over and over again Fonteyn's love of truth gives us rare flashes of beauty.

This young artist's first loyalty is always to the dance; she never gives a performance in the accepted sense, but lives it instead. Because of such an approach the performance is always an exacting experience, both for the public and the artist. Yet she is inevitably restful, for tension is unknown to her mind and her limbs; it is her preoccupation with her performance that we find exacting, for it means that a certain concentration is demanded of us. The response is ungrudging, for the public sense both her demand and the integrity behind it; they feel her serene sincerity, because she has come to terms with herself. Effort that in its final consummation appears to be effortless is a rarity that results in a real understanding between artist and spectator.

It is a fact that her musicality has a great deal to do with her extraordinary co-ordination of mind and movement. Those who have experience of any form of teaching know how the musical sense can unite, and Fonteyn is as musical as she is unified in her approach to movement. But like everything else

70

to do with her work this is felt instinctively by her, conscientiously assessed, and ultimately understood. Her phrasing is technically faultless, and her precision devoid of undue emphasis or showmanship.

Have her dramatic powers been underestimated? Is it not possible that in finding a great dancer we have lost a great actress? The ballet may give her dramatic scope, but drama in ballet tends to play a secondary role. Fonteyn is a great dramatic actress and, incidentally, a very subtle comedienne. How does one judge the acting abilities of a dancer? There is no voice to give light or shade, there are no static moments to register facial expression. One judges such dramatic power by two intricate technicalities. These are the skill and intelligence behind the timing of a movement, and the sensitivity shown towards the amount of emphasis required by a gesture; the gesture may vary in scope from the sudden play of the whole body and face to an isolated movement of a single extremity.

We see real theatre sense when Fonteyn walks towards Hamlet after her parting with Laertes; the angle and the turn of head are so controlled that they emphasise her thoughts, and the slightest exaggeration of either would kill that which she sets out to convey. We can see that her mind and her eyes follow her brother into the distance, although her duty as a daughter compels her to obey Polonius, who leads her in the opposite direction. Watch her tender, solicitous start when Hamlet turns to her with a violence that makes it impossible for her to hide her sudden anxiety; it is here that one senses the fear of misunderstanding rather than the fear of physical violence. The movement is so intelligent, with its subtle timing and its refined control. She can sustain a mood throughout a whole scene— such as her Odette in *Le Lac des Cygnes*—which no intricate step of virtuosity can disturb. Seemingly effortless, welling up from within her, never projected for what it is worth, one knows that in her acting as in her dancing diffusion through every fibre of her body has happened before her audience share anything. One could recall many minor moments to emphasise this side

71

of her work; so much more telling and subtle are they than the most moving of mad scenes in *Giselle*.

Before the company left for its first American tour I said that either Fonteyn would be entirely overlooked or that she would revolutionise the American attitude towards the classical ballerina. Her ultimate triumph did revolutionise their attitude. If she was acceptable to them it could not be otherwise, for she is the personification of lyricism, the English dancer's contribution to the classical ballet. The English dancer's rendering of classical ballet has great lyrical style; it is accompanied by a rare discipline, and a calculated acceptance of the traditional.

Fonteyn, in spite of her youth, is serious and also humorous. I think that it was something underlining this simple fact that moved the Americans. With their enviable quickness of wit and thought, they are very ready to acknowledge a lesson. They analysed and stated the case as they found it with their usual uninhibited generosity.

But every positive has its negative; it would be out of place not to emphasise that all the above rarities demand the full price when the artist concerned is struggling with the isolated bad performance, or with the despondency and lack of inspiration that all experience from time to time. In the former case Fonteyn shows lethargy and lack of attack, and the outline of Ingres-like quality in her work becomes blurred. When she has a spell of the latter's 'No Man's Land' we see a troubled soul that self-condemns but never self-tortures. There is absent the commonplace raillery against fate and personal misfortune; but there is self-criticism, self-abasement and the artist's dissatisfaction with her own progress. Such sufferings on her part are touchingly genuine; any help or understanding offered is not received negatively. Fonteyn takes advice and criticism on such occasions with a wholly receptive mind. Consequently, for her all such moments end in the passing of yet another milestone of learning.

These are the moments when there flashes through my mind the lines of Meredith:

... Faults of feature some see, beauty not complete,
Yet good gossips, beauty that makes holy
Earth and air, may have faults from head to feet.

*   *   *

This article was written over twenty-three years ago, for already by 1951 Margot Fonteyn was a household name across Europe, North America, South America and the Far East. She has, of course, continued to develop as an artist and add to her repertoire, her distinction and her renown. But I leave the above article as I wrote it in 1951—at the time of the onset of her full flowering.

SOPHIE FEDOROVITCH:* An Appreciation

(Published in *The Dancing Times*, 1953)

Sophie Fedorovitch had a very special place in the heart and life of the Sadler's Wells Ballet; she came and went among us without fuss or noisy comment. It was never possible to feel the imposition of will or personality. Yet she knew us all for an unbroken period of twenty-two years, and for the last two years she has been a member of our artistic Advisory Board. It will seem strange and very sad for us to accept the fact that no longer will this quiet figure of strength be seen wandering among her friends in the theatre.

In the early morning Sophie Fedorovitch might be encountered in the paint room, production room or wardrobe room. She could be seen night after night crossing the stage to go in front to watch the performance. She always seemed to be there, ready to answer innumerable questions about costumes. She would seek me out in the office any morning if something disturbed her about a new work. She was a real artist, and she found that life was full. We are all enriched by having

* Sophie Fedorovitch died on January 26th, 1953. *N. de V.*

73

had her for so long in our midst, and in her company one had the feeling that every single day was an important incident— complete in itself.

Many will speak in praise of her work as an artist of the English theatre—but in the history of English ballet her place is unique. The very strength of her own spirit, concerned as it was with true principles, showed over and over again in her creative work for the ballet. The superfluous stroke of the brush would be eliminated as would be the superfluous word. A visual refinement became the outward expression of an inward sense of fastidious values.

Her wisdom was great and her influence far-reaching. Her understanding of ballet design was the outcome of a selfless imposition of study. She had a real knowledge of movement and of the significance of the dancer's lineal expression. She was never known to permit a line or a curve of her design to interfere with or confuse the clarity of the choreography. Her efforts were ceaseless in their search for creative unity.

The Sadler's Wells Ballet, which has the honour in April to produce Sophie Fedorovitch's last ballet designs (for *Veneziana*), has lost a true friend. England has lost a most distinguished theatrical artist, whose influence may well be felt among the younger generation of stage designers for many years to come.

THE ROYAL CHARTER:
A Memorandum
(Submitted in 1954 by Dame Ninette de Valois)

Sometime before the following memorandum was written I had found the ballet situation disturbing. I had discovered that the grants to Sadler's Wells Theatre and the Royal Opera House, Covent Garden, were for the presentation of opera and ballet but not actually for any specific company. The opera at Covent Garden appeared to be in a safe position as it had been created in the building just after the war. There was security also for the Sadler's Wells Opera, but hardly for the two branches of the now 'floating' Sadler's Wells Ballet.

I

I have been asked to prepare a memorandum to be discussed at the special Meeting of Representatives from the Royal Opera House board of directors, the Sadler's Wells Trust, the Sadler's Wells School and the Arts Council of Great Britain.

My reasons for urging a change of name are not based on an immediate problem, nor any feeling of dissatisfaction, but on a view of the future of the Sadler's Wells Ballet—the British National Ballet in all but name. It is a fact that the present

75

Sadler's Wells Ballet, in spite of its position both nationally and internationally, has no individual status and is not organised or recognised as an entity. Its very name at this moment causes much confusion.

The Sadler's Wells Ballet was originally named after two theatres (Vic-Wells), and was then re-named after one theatre (Sadler's Wells). The original company, with its second name, was handed over to Covent Garden in 1945, and a second company was formed at Sadler's Wells, first known as the Sadler's Wells Opera Ballet, and now called the Sadler's Wells Theatre Ballet. At the same time a school, giving general education as well as ballet training, and bearing the same name, was established by the Sadler's Wells Foundation.

It is understandable that today both Covent Garden and Sadler's Wells are embarrassed by the sharing of the name. All parties have recognised that to give one part of this three-fold ballet organisation the name of yet another theatre, the Royal Opera House, would lead to still greater confusion, because:

(a) Sadler's Wells is a world-famous name. For the older company to drop it, embracing as that company does all the ballets and artists that have made the name famous, and hand it back to the younger company, can but prove an embarrassment to the smaller company, and suggest to the theatre public some violent change of policy that does not, and we hope never will, exist.

(b) Both Covent Garden and Sadler's Wells are about to hold an equal interest in the school, and they both look to it for their future dancers.

(c) The integrity, purpose, and possibility of further development of both companies depend on this threefold effort. It is the natural outcome of a carefully planned policy that builds for the future as well as provides for the present. Therefore it would seem clear that the name should embrace the organisation as a whole, rather than be derived from any individual theatre.

The two companies are complementary, and the position of the Sadler's Wells Ballet at Covent Garden is:

(a) There could not have been any full-scale classical ballet presented at Sadler's Wells on the lines that the first company was ready to embark on at the end of the war. This made our transfer inevitable.

(b) The highly specialised ballerina, born to carry on the great traditional ballets, may be partly matured at the Sadler's Wells Theatre, but she can only be developed to her full potentialities in the bigger theatre.

The Sadler's Wells Theatre Ballet's special contributions are:

(a) The opportunity offered to a type of artist particularly suited to modern ballets.

(b) The development of highly talented young dancers who, for many reasons, and usually for their own benefit, cannot always be placed in the bigger company on leaving school.

(c) The production of ballets on a medium-sized scale.

(d) The possibility of experimenting with, and giving experience to young choreographers; this also applies to designers and composers.

It must be added that a close tie and interchange of established artists from both companies should exist in the future. Artists like a variety of roles, and choreographers a change of material to work on; hence the value of one company to the other in their respective creative work.

Thus we can see that to continue, as in the past, to name this enterprise after any one theatre when it serves two, is not practical; while to leave the existing name with two-thirds of the organisation and to re-name the remaining third—which is irrevocably linked with the original name—offers no solution.

It would seem that the names of the two theatres concerned should become a secondary consideration, and that the time has arrived to establish this three-fold institution as a *separate entity under a name which recognises the fundamental unity of the two companies and the school.* Purely as a basis for discussion I suggest the following:

(1) The Royal English Ballet	(a) From the Royal Opera House, Covent Garden.
	(b) From the Sadler's Wells Theatre.
(2) The Royal Ballet	ditto
(3) The Royal National Ballet	ditto
(4) The Royal National Ballet of Great Britain	ditto
(5) The Royal British Ballet	ditto
(6) The Royal Commonwealth Ballet	ditto

III

I feel it important to stress my reasons for making a request for a change of name at this moment. I do so as the founder of the companies and not as their present director. The question of a name is but a first step in a plan that would enable our ballet to face its existence as an *entity*, and so ensure its continuity whatever conditions may prevail.

The existence of ballet and opera, housed under one roof, has been an historical fact for nearly three hundred years, and therefore we should recognise that there is a sound policy behind the arrangement. Both the Sadler's Wells Ballet Companies have had the best possible treatment and consideration shown to them by their respective managements, and it is clear that there is a great deal to be said for the existing arrangement. Yet I am anxious, since our ballet tradition is so new, that all drifting without a definite *protective* policy for the future should cease. It is clear that my reasons should be placed before the present group of people who are concerned with our artistic and economic welfare.

The following points need consideration:

(a) Ballet is less expensive to run, and is also a far greater earner of money than opera.

(b) Should there be in the future any heavy cut in subsidies, the ballet could bear this far more easily than the opera.

(c) As long as our artists receive the treatment and encouragement that they do at present, and our artistic standard is maintained, it is not our concern if the greater part of the subsidy is spent on the more complicated sister art. I must underline that this is not a question of a quarrel between opera and ballet, but of realistic thinking.

I do, however, feel concerned when heavy commercial work is undertaken by the ballet, and the profits (over and above the subsidy) are used to cover opera losses. The reasons for my concern are:

(a) No part of these outside earnings is sunk in the ballet's rather needy foundations.

(b) We do this work with no recognition of our entity as a unit, and no reckoning as to our future status in the event of any major financial disaster.

(c) Dancers' salaries are modest in comparison with those of singers. This would be fair enough if we had a proper pension scheme, but the one in existence at the moment is purely a charitable affair.

IV

My appeal is that we face these problems, and find a solution that will make our loyalties to the present managements even stronger. I ask your indulgence towards my anxiety to protect the ballet's and the individual artist's birthright.

It seems to me that it is important, if we are to have a clear picture, for the Arts Council to get a rough summary of our running expenses on paper, that is, of those items that can be separated from the opera. Examples:

Debit: (a) Yearly Salaries.

(b) Orchestra per annual performances and scheduled number of rehearsals.

(c) Production costs, including designers' and composers' fees, wardrobe and general production costs for special works mounted over a period of two years (to strike an average per annum).

Credit: (a) Takings for one whole season (stating number of performances both in London and on tour).

(b) Statement of profits from an American tour. As this happens approximately every three years, an average of what it is worth per annum should be taken into consideration.

By this means an idea could at least be gained as to what an annual subsidy for the ballet alone might mean, should such an event become inevitable.

To sum up: the solution of the name problem is a first logical step towards the recognition of the two companies and the school as an entity, a recognition essential to its preservation and growth. While a change in the present system may not be urgent, it is well to have a plan for the future when the people of understanding who have watched and helped in the growth of the ballet are no longer concerned with its welfare.

I would add again that I speak of a period in the history of our national ballet that may never concern me personally and that I state the case as I see it today, with the eyes of its founder and not of its present director.

The above memorandum was sympathetically discussed by the various representative directors concerned. At the end of the meeting I expressed the view that 'the ballet did not exist ...'

Some weeks later our chairman, Viscount Waverley, met me and told me that I had been right; the ballet companies did not in actual fact exist, and this had made difficulties for him in the application for a Charter; but the matter had been helped by the fact that the ballet school was a Limited Company. He added, 'This is proving to be a very intriguing little document.'

Another board had to be set up to meet with this contingency, it was named the Royal Ballet Board of Directors.

THE ENGLISH BALLET

(A paper by Dame Ninette de Valois, D.B.E.,
director of the Royal Ballet, read to the Royal
Society of Arts on Wednesday, 29th May 1957,
with Sir Arthur Bliss, Master of the Queen's
Musick, in the Chair.)

I have the honour this afternoon to address the Royal Society
of Arts; this important and happy occasion for me has coincided
with many celebrations in connection with the twenty-fifth
birthday of the Royal Ballet. I thus wish to express—on behalf
of myself and the Royal Ballet—that we feel your tribute is a
particularly gracious one.

It is now possible to see that, in the last twenty-five years,
the ballet as a branch of our cultural life in the theatre has travelled a very great distance. I can only dare to touch on the
fringe of the matter; for the shaping of the whole is still so much
in the making. The pattern is by no means complete enough
for me to analyse its finer points; there is an element in it of
shifting sand. To arrest its progress at any point is out of the
question; it must be permitted, in fact encouraged, to press forward. At this moment in the history of English ballet, the
faintest sign of complacency is not permissible.

It has often struck me that when the masques (that great form
of English theatrical art of the earlier centuries) disintegrated,
the English dance fell by the wayside; it did not succeed in

establishing itself as a complete art form of the lyric theatre as soon as the opera and the drama.

Let us now realise what has happened: the ballet has at last acquired in England a status of equality in the theatre with that of drama and music.

There is one further recognition of importance at this point. Its healthy economic, as well as artistic, position in the theatre today, finds it able to demand, on terms of equality, the services of both men and women.

The decline of the status of ballet in Europe towards the end of the nineteenth century resulted (particularly in England, with its lack of any ballet tradition) in some outstandingly depressing conventions. The most outrageous of these conventions was the fact that we hardly recognised the existence of the male dancer. This remarkable attitude continued until the advent of the Diaghilev Russian Ballet at Drury Lane in 1909; this was an event in the history of the theatre that swept us off our feet; it eventually dispelled our state of mental stagnation towards the art of the ballet in the English theatre.

Time has spoken for us: today it is a fact that the Royal Ballet alone has, in the last few years, supplied some of the leading national opera houses in Europe with ballet masters and male choreographers. We are returning to the golden age of ballet again with one of its original truths reaffirmed, namely, the proper emphasis on the male choreographer, dancer and ballet master.

All the above remarks tempt me to speak of something that is not generally known, and that is the source of the ballet's fundamental roots. I feel sure that many people are convinced of its inherent artificiality; its divorce from any form of natural dance movement. Nothing, though, could be further from the truth; it is a fact that all the ballet's fundamental dance steps are derived from the folk dances of Western Europe.

The significance and importance of this is far-reaching; in consequence there can be traced, from the Basque country to the Highlands of Scotland, not only the steps but the very style of the classical dance. I know of no pastime that gives me more delight than to witness the annual display of folk dancing at the Albert Hall; I am able to recognise and name, according to the academic terminology of the classical ballet, every step that I see executed. Here I see these steps unadorned, yet neatly executed in their original simple form. It should be known that Western European dance masters lifted many of the actual dances wholesale into the theatre, and the steps were heightened in their execution; in the end they were developed into their present state of perfection. This effort must have been achieved by a fascinating process of working backwards. The early ballet masters, in their searchings for the perfecting and further development of folk dance steps, seem to have turned their attention to the anatomical structure of the human form. By studying the body and the limbs they evolved exercises (many of them based on existing simple dance movements) that scientifically developed the general physique of the dancer. Thus a finer instrument was modelled as a means to help towards a more intricate rendering of existing dance steps.

Such painstaking research work eventually resulted in three great schools of ballet in the Western European theatre; schools that are known today as the French, Italian and Danish: they are the result of the pooled resources of the folk dance steps of Europe. Each country eventually evolved its particular individual school or 'style', developing, over a period of time, its own markedly national form of creative self-expression in the theatre.

The English school had now sprung into existence, basically through contact with the French, Italian and Danish schools: it again is evolving its own particular style.

I feel that you want me to speak of the great Russian school of ballet. Russian ballet again sprang originally from the classicism of Western Europe. It has since evolved its own very definite style, both theatrically and academically speaking. The style is very marked and shows its influence as far afield as Poland, Hungary and Czechoslovakia. This Russian school

84

should today be recognised as the classical ballet in Eastern Europe.

We must now consider the true relationship of the English ballet, and the possibility of any really marked influence at work. I would say, in speaking of the present-day pedagogy in Russia itself, that the influence is not very strong. If we speak, though, of certain *international* influences, it is another matter: as an example, the influence of the Russian ballet in Western Europe as personified in the Diaghilev Russian Ballet. Here is the one great influence; for in this particular case, we speak of the main guiding force on the artistic and creative approach of the English ballet in the theatre. Russian ballet in Western Europe has become the guiding star of our theatre tradition.

I have already stressed the pooling of Western Europe's national dances as the classical ballet's foundation; we should remind ourselves that our own native dances have played their part—notably in the style of Scottish dancing, where the traditional grouping of the fingers is to be found as a convention in all the early classical schools. So when we speak of the general 'style' of our classical dancing, we are able to prove that it has been attained through this general European heritage. We have, therefore, naturally more in common with the French, Italian and Danish schools than the Russian school of today. Why is this so? Did not the Russian school also inherit classicism from the great schools of the West? Certainly, as its foundation; but Russian ballet has been in the theatre for many years. Consider therein certain Eastern influences; consider, for the moment, the difference that there is to be found in the folk dance of Eastern Europe with its strong dynamic rhythms and movement that liberates the whole body; it shows itself to be far removed from the impeccable precision and neatness that we associate with Western movement in folk dance. Therefore, through the influence of Slav folk dance in all Eastern European creative work, it is but a step later to the development of a more plastique classicism, a classicism that is now peculiarly their

85

own and more in keeping with the Eastern strain that is ever present in the Slav races.

We belong to Western Europe; to change our 'style' would be to kill our particular individuality, and to confuse the issue of our future place in the history of dancing.

I must emphasise, though, that 'style' must not be confused with certain more scientific principles and findings that are the natural heritage of the international side of any national school. There will always exist certain major discoveries that are destined to be shared by all; such findings become important contributions to the general progress of ballet in all countries.

So much for our foundations. What has actually been achieved in the last twenty-five years? I emphasise once again that a strong position has been obtained within our theatre life, and within the last decade there has also been a considerable international recognition bestowed on us. It is the first time in the history of this country's lyric theatre that a national ballet is acclaimed as a serious means of showing the life of our people in yet another national art-form.

Our very youthful existence points to a state that has demanded of us in the past a marked degree of caution; the time factor involved has meant that the challenge of 'neglect' on our part in certain directions of development is not without foundation. Our present caution springs from our obsession with fundamentals; we have been to date rightly concerned with a certain international attitude in our approach to the academic as well as the theatrical side of our ballets. It is wise to put all that we have inherited from the past to the test before we attempt to discard anything in part.

Today it can be said that the English school has by now absorbed classicism in the main; it is moving forward to a second stage, for it is already showing signs of creating its own interpretation of established traditional classical ballet of international fame and usage. Its own creative work, of a more international order, bears the stamp of the neo-classicism as expressed in so many works of the Diaghilev ballet of yesterday and the French school of today. What of our more truly national choreography?

Here England has a greater problem. Perhaps it has been a little understandable that a country with no balletic history has turned, in its first efforts, to its literature rather more than its individual folk dance for inspiration. Again, in our painting the narrative element that is so often to be found here, has resulted in our school of painting acting as a strong national inspiration for our ballets. I feel that we have yet to solve the problem of our folk dance and its place in the theatre; that is to say, the problem of its recognition in our theatre ballets. Certain folk dance and folk lore ballets are necessary in every national ballet company; they should be fostered if only to develop the special characteristics of the native dancer; such works are a sure means of expressing a country's national form of musicality.

The English dancer has shown himself to possess neatness, speed and precision in his technical feats. In his more expressive moments we are aware that he has a marked lyrical quality; in his dramatisation of a scene is shown a strong sense of detailed characterisation.

We await a further generation of English dancers emerging from their own newly-founded tradition; it is inevitable that this future generation of artists will bring forth some young choreographers bent on a more distinctly national form of self-expression.

Since the opening of the Royal Covent Garden Opera House in 1946, it has been the task of the Royal Ballet to establish a national ballet on the grand scale in our country, and we have, very naturally, modelled much of our effort on all the work that has preceded our existence in the form of other national ballets. I have said though, that our own future style is much in evidence; our task in the immediate future is to develop what is there and bend it to our will.

Creatively speaking, in the theatre the English school has followed the modern conception of ballet (again a heritage of

87

Diaghilev) in the form of emphasis on the completely self-contained one-act ballet.

This form, in its purest conception, was born about forty years ago; at that time it was welcomed as an effort to re-establish the greater principles of choreography, including that of its relationship to the better forms of music; the timely birth of this new order spelt the death knell of the numerous elongated, decadent and musically insignificant ballets of the late nineteenth century. We are today left only with the few surviving masterpieces of that time. The highly concentrated one-act ballet did much to embellish and widen choreography—particularly in the sphere of modern experimental work. It is the basis of the English theatre school; although we have familiarised ourselves with the handful of the great classics that have survived the last century, we are still unfamiliar with the basic handling of full-length ballet in creative work.

My recent visit to Moscow showed me that, although we needed a complete understanding of the approach to the three-act work, Russia was much in need of the reverse—the one-act ballet of Western Europe. During my stay in Moscow, the Russians expressed to me their wish that we should bring over to Russia many of our one-act ballets.

In England, I feel very strongly that we need the experiment in creative production of the more spacious, leisured approach; we need contact with that forgotten part of the theatre in modern ballet—the part that I can only describe as theatre-sense; it lies at the core of these great traditional three-act ballets. The structure of the scenario alone is of immense importance, for never does it appear to be an obscure peg used to hang movement on; it becomes, instead, a *raison d'être* for movement itself, a return to the significance of drama in the theatre.

In Russia today though, through no experimental developments and an over-emphasis on what we lack, there is evidence of the disintegration of true choreography; there were many examples to be seen of choreography as a mere serving-maid of the narrative, reducing, in many cases, the dance scenes to a series of banal dance clichés. Russia appears to need the taut, relentless demand of pure, undiluted choreography: the form of choreography that becomes a pure abstraction in its demand for a complete dedication of movement for movement's sake. Thus we both (England and Russia) have much to learn if we submit to a disciplined temporary dedication to that theatre form that is weakest in our own respective creative work.

Only in *The Prince of the Pagodas* have we in England, so far, attempted an experiment in the full-length medium of ballet, where all may be said to have been completely started from scratch. Neither the scenario, the music, nor the choreography was in existence two years ago.

Benjamin Britten has been the first English composer to attempt this disciplined medium of composition for the ballet: he did so with enthusiasm and understanding and contributed by far the most mature effort on the overall creative side. His efforts produced, in the process, moments of great beauty in the score.

We are holding ourselves responsible for a second full-length work, commissioned as a whole, for production early in 1958. It will be on the subject matter of *Ondine*—and the creation of Mr Frederick Ashton, in conjunction with Hans Werner Henze, the German composer, and Miss Lila de Nobili, the Italian artist.

I have touched in general on our position in the world today as a recognised national ballet. Twenty-five years of life is very young in comparison with the great national companies of long standing. Ballet criticism in this country is, of course, even younger. A national ballet has to be created before the advent of the ballet critics; it cannot be considered possible to achieve really mature ballet criticism for yet another fifteen years. We would be wanting, however, in generosity and understanding if we expected things to be otherwise. These critics of ours have no national heritage to guide them and very little space allotted to them in the Press. Nevertheless, the thankless responsibility of assuming the burden of this task is something that must be attempted, otherwise no real progress will ever be made. Some of these critics, of course, regard attack as the best means of defence. On thinking it over—why not? There are less vital ways of standing up to the painful business of acquiring knowledge.

PHASE III

The 1960s and the 1970s

The 1960s and the 1970s

In the year 1963 I retired and was replaced by Sir Frederick Ashton, who had been my associate director for many years.

The Establishment continued to develop in various directions. Before I retired we visited Russia, and a little later Nureyev joined our company as a permanent guest artist and became Margot Fonteyn's principal partner. Immense studio space was developed at Baron's Court housing the Royal Ballet Upper School and the Royal Ballet with its three groups: the Covent Garden Company, the Touring Group and 'Ballet for All'.

There were two notable developments:

(1)　The introduction of a proper study in the Lower School of our national and folk dances. This venture is meeting with a real sign of general interest and appreciation.

(2)　The Benesh System of Notation first started by the Royal Ballet becomes the Institute of Choreology with an Arts Council Grant. It receives wide recognition among ballet companies in general.

By the latter half of this period the Royal Ballet produces a new group of star dancers, both male and female. Anthony Dowell, David Wall, Michael Coleman, Wayne Sleep, Antoinette Sibley, Merle Park, Lynn Seymour, Monica Mason, Leslie Collier, Margaret Barbieri.

In 1970, the Royal Ballet appoints, on the retirement of Ash-

93

ton, their third director over a period of forty years—Kenneth MacMillan.

What of the future? The final test of any achievement lies in its survival. I bow out with the guilty feeling that I have had the most exciting, stimulating and rewarding part to play in this story of our Establishment. Strange as it seems, time could show that my task may prove itself to have been the easiest.

The articles in this particular phase deal mainly with the influences on the development of the Royal Ballet in general, and have been written over a period of about twelve years.

GEMINI: TWO STUDIES

Reason is the enumeration of quantities already known; imagination is the perception of the values of these quantities, both separately and as a whole.

Shelley

JOHN CRANKO

. . . To each his world is private,
and in that world one excellent minute.
And in that world one tragic minute
These arc private.

Yevtushenko, from his poem 'People'

Two Royal Ballet choreographers are forever twinned in my memory. They are John Cranko, who died in the summer of 1973, and the present director of the Royal Ballet, Kenneth MacMillan.

Both were at work in the company during the late 1940s and both served for some years as dancers and then as choreographers. John was the elder; he came to us from South Africa, the country that poured so much talent into England during our first four years at Covent Garden. Kenneth graduated from the Royal Ballet School and was a strong young classical dancer in the making.

They were always great friends, and there sprang up between

them a mutual admiration society. Both of them had generous natures, and neither suffered any pangs of jealousy about the other. For several years Kenneth was often seen dancing for John. I can remember him appearing in a new choreographic venture of John's in the little theatre at Henley-on-Thames, for John was never still and worked incessantly outside the Royal Ballet when not fully occupied choreographically within it. I remember John saying to me some years later—when we were having one of those inexplicable unproductive choreographic patches among the younger school—'Well, thank goodness there's Kenneth.'

Both were, in turn, during their early years when with us, resident choreographers for some time to the touring section of the Royal Ballet. Both, understandably if regrettably, had to take themselves elsewhere at a later date for further development and more opportunities.

The only likeness in their work is the shared schooling and the tradition. Both we can claim to be Royal Ballet products, and neither ever thought or wished at any time that he could have had it otherwise. I say 'only likeness', but it is an important one, as it stands for a certain stability of outlook that should be preserved. It is an establishment root that may appear in its essence to be intangible, and consequently not easily recognised in their respective creative productions—but nevertheless it is there in the form of a birthmark or tattoo—whichever symbol you prefer to use.

The friendship and interest in each other's work continued after they had left the Royal Ballet. There were choreographic interchanges between Stuttgart (Cranko) and Berlin (MacMillan), and earlier, before Kenneth had left London and when John was already in Stuttgart, he invited Kenneth to work out there. Kenneth's much admired rendering of Mahler's 'Song of the Earth' had its first presentation through the generosity of his friend, for when the Covent Garden board of the 1950s decided against the production for musical reasons, Stuttgart immediately invited Kenneth to mount it.

It is of John, though, that I wish to speak here. I write of him with a sense of great loss, but I must add with just as much pride, for his career as the choreographic director of the company lasted for fourteen years.

I remember first his remarkable intelligence, his fantastic sense of comedy, both subtle and slapstick, and his gift for tragi-comedy. There was always present vitality and a sense of enterprise.

He was a wonderful companion, someone that I loved to talk to when I was feeling exhausted. Just before one of our big American tours I can remember a long, swift car drive with him to Aldeburgh to visit Benjamin Britten and to listen to the score of *The Prince of the Pagodas*. The whole day seemed alive with John's youthful optimism and purpose; there seemed to be no reason for any tentative feelings about embarking on the first full-length English ballet.

I thought highly of this work and still do—both musically and choreographically. If it had been produced in Russia there would have been oceans of leisurely time both in the rehearsal room and on the stage before and after the event. Time to smooth out any rough passages, to prune where necessary, and to rethink all the inevitable moments of weakness in a work of such length; time for the composer and the choreographer to get together and reconstruct certain scenes. That it is not possible to find this time in England is one of the major tragedies of the English ballet scene. As usual in state opera houses, the time factor and the mad forward planning—to accommodate guest stars, their dates and their agents—make creative rethinking an impossibility. This ballet in its original form is lost to us, for the Benesh Notation was not fully installed at that time, and consequently it was never notated. But we must realise that in the history of the British ballet *The Prince of the Pagodas* is a very important work: the first full-length ballet score by such a distinguished composer as Benjamin Britten, and a work commissioned for an English choreographer. It is all there to be rechoreographed, and this is of greater urgency than half a dozen more versions of *The Sleeping Beauty* (or *The Sleep-Walking Prince*, as it shows signs of becoming).

Watching John's *Onegin* during the Stuttgart Ballet's season at Covent Garden in 1974, one was struck with his highly developed sense of theatre. In the past, to keep himself fully occupied, he wisely did a good deal of commercial work, and in such work a neat balancing of the whole is demanded. This has nothing to do with 'talent' in the more isolated sense of the word, it is good craftsmanship that is always demanded in all such forms of production work. He proved himself to be a real craftsman, and the mind flies at once to the miniature perfection of *Pineapple Poll* and other early efforts.

Again, I admired *Antigone;* it, too, should have had some proper revision, further stage rehearsals and readjustments. But no publication of a revised edition was forthcoming although everything about the ballet called for a final effort, an effort that would have not over-strained anybody. It might well have turned it into a one-act masterpiece, particularly when it was so well served by its decor, music and scenario.

At first, John Cranko had no ties with any particular country except England; until he settled in Germany he was a Commonwealth pioneer, whether in various sides of the theatre or in various parts of the country. Like all such artists he could be found from time to time in a self-inflicted no-man's land. It was never really anything more than the natural wanderlust of a frustrated extrovert, for his observations, interests and adventures were wide and varied, and at times equally hasty in their conception and untidy in their execution.

He loved and responded whole-heartedly to music and his taste here was very catholic; he was never overawed by any music score and consequently he was sometimes pretty reckless as to what use he put it to. His vitality and sense of adventure were very much in evidence during the years of his early development, and it was very much wanted in the ballet theatre world at that time. He always took a serious interest in the progress of the students, and found time when he was with us to experiment with some choreographic classes of his own construction. He was aware of the importance of schooling, and after he left us he used to send special students to the Royal Ballet School for one or two years' study. When he persuaded the Stuttgart authorities to let him have a boarding school attached to the Ballet School, immediately there came to the Royal Ballet Junior Branch at White Lodge teachers to study our methods in general.

I saw him for the last time when he came to have dinner with me some years ago. He told me that when he was in a jam about something he found himself saying, 'Now what did Madam do in such a case?' He would remember and do likewise. 'But,' he added, laughing, 'I was among the first to say on such occasions—"Oh hell! She's gone too far this time!"—yet today I find myself inevitably acting the same way.'

He did not make enemies for he had not got that sort of nature. His fellow artists loved him and worked for him with enthusiasm.

His death at forty-five was a tragedy. His reconstruction of the Stuttgart Ballet will be a part of the history of the European ballet scene for many a long year. It was here that he fought apathy on a grand scale and conquered it. Perhaps this was the challenge that he needed: to have to create something to create from.

Before he left for Germany he had been through a period of adverse—in fact almost hostile—criticism. A period that anyone with abilities well over the average has to go through at some time in a career. I can remember how difficult it was for me to persuade Sol Hurok to include some of John's ballets in our New York repertoire. I won the argument, but the critics had their own adverse say on the matter.

During Cranko's later visits to the States with his own company, we read of 'standing ovations'. America accepts slowly choreographic works from elsewhere. Some of their past choreographic criticisms of the Royal Ballet's repertoire makes interesting reading in the light of the very same works' success today.

In comparison with any other choreographer since the war, it might be said that he worked twice as hard and at twice the speed coupled with infinitely more responsibilities. It was almost as if something was telling him that time was not on his side ...

Perhaps he gave everything that he had in the onrush; perhaps we can comfort ourselves with the thought that we have with us now the golden era of John Cranko.

KENNETH MACMILLAN

'The Quality of Mercy is not strained ...'

Shakespeare

Kenneth MacMillan is a product of the Royal Ballet School and Company. Unlike other English choreographers he was, when young, a gifted classical dancer with a strong technique. He took over the directorship of the Royal Ballet on the retirement of Sir Frederick Ashton in 1970. I think that everyone saw the inevitability of this choice, particularly in view of his already well known and highly successful choreographic works both for the Royal Ballet and other companies.

Understandably, he has had to combat the usual diverse opinions that such decisions involve. Better, though, to live through controversy than to exist in an atmosphere of apathy.

MacMillan was not born a Scotsman for nothing. On the surface I do not know a more reserved, unspectacular and sensitive person, nor do I know a more sincere, granite-like character underneath. He states his case quietly and refuses to embroider it, nor does he ever turn up the hem neatly and fix it once and for all. For a certain section of the public he will always remain an enigma; to those who know him well and believe in his great gifts, first and foremost they must show patience and understanding. He has his own world, and within this world he lives, works and thinks. Small talk is unknown to him; if he has nothing to say of any interest he remains silent, aloof from the nattering ebb and flow, and totally unaware that his self-removal may be causing some embarrassment. All his statements are simple, whether about life or the ballet. I once praised his excellent cooking. 'Well,' he said, 'I ought to be able to do it, my father was a chef and my mother was a cook.'

He shares John Cranko's background, as already stated: a product of our classical school with its form and heritage ever present even in his experimental works. His range is wide, overflowing with choreographic speculation and subtle musicality. Some of our dancers once told me that a new MacMillan ballet presented no fresh problems to them at the first orchestral rehearsal. In other words, the choreographer detects all that has to be digested in the score and weaves his choreography around it. This approach is highlighted in the brilliant court dances in Act II of *Anastasia*, and again in *The Rite of Spring*.

A certain weakness springs, inevitably, from the very great facility of his choreographic invention. There is occasionally a lack of development in his themes, and again his bridging and general stagecraft need momentary attention; a dazzling flow of inventive movement often offers no judicious respite from itself. Of course this is not generally the case, for there are many ballets of his that have succeeded in every aspect of their presentation. I am dwelling on some of his contemporary and more exciting choreography that has not yet turned into the unified, well-defined statement that it will be. Here we have the perfect example of a choreographer who can benefit from periods of revision after the production of a major work of length and complexity. His major works are on the grand scale, and that is rare today.

As an established choreographer he naturally has his own style of dancer as others have had in the past. We speak of Balanchine dancers (and Balanchine speaks of Petipa dancers), Ashton dancers, Cranko dancers, Béjart dancers and we also speak of MacMillan dancers. His choreographic form is definitely accepted, and this is one of the marks of a choreographer who has arrived.

It is as well to remember that it takes more than half the period of a choreographer's career to state his case on a scale that makes a fair judgement possible for posterity. MacMillan is some thirty years younger than the most prominent modern names in our repertoire; he has been choreographing for almost twenty-five years as against their fifty years of work.

He has a shrewd grasp of the general standard of execution that will be needed to play the required part in the future development of the company. There is to be noticed a moulding of the Royal Ballet in progress as it moves into the next phase of its existence. This must be, for to stand still, however skilfully, would be to court disaster. This forward-looking aspect is happening under the direction of a comparatively young man, and at a random moment when form in the theatre is going through a desultory period in general, and the Royal Ballet itself is faced with having to adjust itself to the generation gap within its own personal world. A time indeed of flux and change.

But if things were not this way we would be a dying effort. MacMillan and his generation are confronted with the demands of today and the paying of the correct amount of homage to yesterday. We must note that as for the dancers in the company the situation is likewise for the choreographers: a ceaseless competition against what has already been achieved, and the ever present challenge of the next development.

Our audiences are sharply divided. There are the balletomanes who find the ballets of Minkus as potent as marjoram; the nostalgic ones that seek out the rather mummified modernity of the late twenties and thirties; but ever present also is the public that possesses a sense of proportion, discrimination and an uncontaminated interest. All this is in the shape of a natural evolution, but it does not make the task any easier.

This is Kenneth MacMillan's world. An artist whose heritage and forward-looking inclination necessitate that he keeps one foot in the past and places the other in the future. Meanwhile, life demands that he should balance the present and complete the Gemini pattern.

THE STRANGER IN OUR MIDST

Towards the billowy freedom
Of the green open sea
Sails a multitude of ships
White are their sails.

And among all these ships
Moves my own little boat;
A boat which has no sails,
Only a pair of sculls ...

Lermontov

It was quite by chance that, on a visit to Leningrad, I saw a young man make his first appearance in a ballet called *Laurencia*, dancing with the famous Natalia Dudinskaya. His name was Rudolf Nureyev. He recalls me coming into Pushkin's male dancers' class, at the Kirov school. 'But you did not stay to see us,' he adds. 'You went straight through to another class.'

We were fated not to meet in Leningrad. But later, when the Royal Ballet was performing there at the Kirov Theatre and the Kirov Company was on its way to dance in London, Rudi took matters into his own hands. The episode of his defection in Paris was not mentioned in Leningrad. We only learned the facts when we returned to London.

A few months later I was to see him dance in London at a Gala performance on the stage of The Theatre Royal, Drury Lane. The dances that he executed on this occasion left me dissatisfied. I did not feel that they told me anything about the dancer. Eventually he took his bows in front of the red curtain. I saw an arm raised with a noble dignity, a hand expressively extended with that restrained discipline which is the product of a great traditional schooling. Slowly the head turned from one side of the theatre to the other, and the Slav bone-structure of the face, so beautifully modelled, made me feel like an inspired sculptor rather than the director of the Royal Ballet. I could see him suddenly and clearly in one role—Albrecht in *Giselle*. Then and there I decided that when he first danced for us it must be with Fonteyn in that ballet. When, many months later, I told him of my swift decision he looked very solemn. 'That,' he said, 'must go into a book.' Well, here it is.

At the end of a long career in the ballet world one looks back on those past moments that have been unforgettably inspiring. They are few, and more than often widely separated. Nureyev's portrayal of Albrecht is one of mine. To see him dance this role shortly after my decision was to experience everything I sensed in that raised arm and turn of the head. It was a deeply thoughtful and credible interpretation.

No Russian can shake off the soil of his country. Even if they live and work abroad for years they seem to carry around with them their own cage of escapism into which they suddenly dive. From there they will regard with a broody or violent disdain that foreign, outside world which they may well have deliberately chosen.

Rudi was no exception, and I learned to know the signs. When it happened it was like watching a panther at bay—so much at bay that even the pride of self-control was no more. Such outbursts were, I know, as painful for him as for us. They were also confusing—for never could one forget that he had, fundamentally, a true sense of humility about himself and his art. At this stage of his career his integrity, dedication and exu-

104

berance were allied to a youthful innocence that animated his dancing with something of the concentration of a child in its own special world.

I recall one evening during his first visit. He was not dancing, but rehearsing movements out of *Giselle* alone on the stage. It was six o'clock, and a worried ballet master asked me if I would stop him as they had to have the stage for a last-minute rehearsal. I went up to him and explained that he would have to leave the stage, but could come back in half an hour. He gave in at once; but looking at me solemnly he said: 'Yes, I come back. But the mood, the mood it will have gone ...'

It was not a grumble, or a merely selfish reaction; it was to him a painful fact. He was acutely aware that something he had just found was about to be lost, and that maybe he would never be able to recover it. It should be further noted that this was *after* his first performance with us.

How does one learn to know artists? By watching them at work, privately as well as publicly, by talking to them and listening to them talking. But even more important may be the brief reflections expressed by them on matters outside their own highly specialised world. I once asked Rudi about a country he had visited, and where he had met with particular acclaim. 'It is sick,' was his only brief comment.

His approach to life in the West was very thorough, for he is highly intelligent and blessed with a subtle sense of humour and a keen curiosity. We once had a fierce argument about looking for a balance between security and freedom. When I had finished, I received a long grave look, and then: 'Say it all again, Madam—in little words, please.'

He came among us from a very different life and a very different repertoire of ballets. He had no knowledge of modern ballet in the neo-classical sense, nor had he danced to any really modern music. But in the six years that he had been attached, first to the Kirov School and then to the Kirov, he had managed to absorb an astonishing knowledge of the classical choreography. In his one-act production of *La Bayadère*, the first work he mounted for the Royal Ballet, we have a beautifully constructed reproduction, executed with taste and care. Petipa has never been better served. Nureyev has given the artists of the Royal Ballet the very spirit of this great French choreographer.

He got the very best traditional classical work out of our dancers on this occasion. In fact, I afterwards found the Kirov production disappointing in comparison. (Such a paradox is not uncommon. For instance, when Anton Dolin mounted his *Pas de Quatre* on the Kirov Company, I found their style and execution of this work far surpassed any English version I had seen.)

The other productions of his that I know, notably *The Nutcracker* and his first *Raymonda*, show that he has still a great deal to learn about production and the 'bridging' of his scenes; but they are rich and competent in their skilful adaptation and development of classical choreographic steps and patterns already known to him, and in many cases there are interesting flashes of his own choreography. I am a great admirer of his *Nutcracker*, although the production may well be considered on the heavy side in comparison with other versions. But the choreography whether his or his inheritance never fails to please me, and his musical phrasing in movements like the big 'Snowflakes' number is subtle and interesting.

This brings me to the question of his musicality. Some are inclined to doubt its existence because of his undisciplined demands for ill-chosen *tempi* for some traditional dances. But we must not forget that he comes from a school that permits such liberties to be taken with the old classical ballets. We must judge him by what happens when he is faced with a modern score. What does happen? He makes his usual approach—a mixture of concentration, humility, and respect for anything 'new'. A new problem is not a waste of time to Nureyev; it is a serious matter for application and understanding.

The phenomenal speed with which he learns a new role cannot be put down only to technique and a good memory; it is based on his instinctive musicality and his wonderful academic schooling. Of course there is always present the difference between the precision of the Western classical school and the wider sweep and more lethargic approach of Eastern Europe. I have seen him attack and conquer with remarkable ease a difficult modern abstract ballet of today, only to sense also that he had difficulty with an apparently simple Bournonville variation, or with the Knight's dance in my own *Checkmate*. Always, though, the intelligence and the demanding love to understand is there. 'I will do it well one day, but not yet.' Never, 'It is not worth trying.'

His dancing does not by any means sweep the performances of other male dancers off the stage, as some of his more fanatical admirers would have it. But we must accept in him the quality of stardom—the inner fire, whether in a male or female performer, which surmounts the usual standards of criticism scrutinising each separate facet of a performance. It has been said that trifles make perfection, but perfection is no trifle. There is a lot of truth in that old cliché, and there comes to my mind the remark of Maestro Enrico Cecchetti when he spoke of Anna Pavlova. 'People ask me about her; I say she has genius, and I add that you cannot explain genius—you accept it.'

What has Rudolf Nureyev done for the West? We know that we have opened his eyes to many things; we have led him up new paths, widened his horizon and imposed some self-discipline on him. These are the very experiences he came to us to seek. What have we received in return? I would say, to use a terse and down to earth expression, that we received a strong 'shot in the arm'. No longer is the male dancer in the great classics a secondary figure, whose support of the ballerina counts far more than his own performance. There is now a true partnership with the male knowing that his dancing, his acting and his work with the ballerina are of equal status with hers. This important redistribution of effort is something we have to thank him for, and the English ballet scene took this very much to heart. To this day, the younger school of male dancers are ungrudging in their praise for him on this point, and the young ballerinas never fail to find the challenge anything but an inspiration; for he never supplants his partner, he always carries her along with him.

This brings me closer to his famous partnership with Margot Fonteyn. By 1961 Fonteyn had reached a difficult stage in her career. It was the time when she found herself without Robert Helpmann or Michael Somes to work with—two justly famous fellow artists who had proved themselves to be devoted and highly skilled partners of many years' standing. She had reached an age when a change of partnership was not an easy matter for her. Young as he was, Nureyev proved to be the answer; he, on his side, was fortunate that during the first tentative years of his self-imposed exile he should find that this famous dancer was to prove herself an inspiring and understanding friend. Quick to sense each other's intelligence, and quick to grasp what they could do for each other, their partnership blossomed into a face lift for England's Royal Ballet.

With the exception of the great classics, there seemed very few works in our repertoire that were suited to Nureyev when he first came to England. But I was impressed from the first by his determination to master the choreographic context that he found here. He appeared determined to study and dance any role, big or small, whether or not there were the opportunities present to display his technical powers. Of such stuff are great artists made, and by such measurements are we able to judge the sincerity of Nureyev's approach to his new world.

He must have felt the change from the breadth and attack that exists in all traditional Russian choreography. An immense amount of intricate detail is packed into every part of Western choreography, and therefore it demands a greater understanding and discipline on the part of the performer. Our Western theatre stages are smaller than the Russian, the theatres themselves more intimate; and so, for the stranger, our whole approach must have given a feeling of congestion. With us the moments of high choreographic beauty do not so boldly assert themselves; they have to be discovered, studied and more slowly perfected.

I have never accepted the attitude that Nureyev should wholly 'fit into' the Royal Ballet. When he dances the classics we are more aware of the difference between the Russian style and ours than when we actually see a whole Russian company dancing together. The individual performance is intensely interesting for the artists, it gives them the opportunity to note highlights which they may blend into their own interpretations without destroying their personal style.

But Nureyev, with his restless, searching mind and his wonderful background, which nevertheless in the end forced him to feel that he must seek for expansion outside, provides inevitably a portrait of an isolated individual. Not many of us have had the experience of suddenly cutting ourselves adrift, sacrificing things that have a place at the core of our being. Such a drastic action is not necessarily a calculated act of courage. It can be the outcome of a despairing frustration not even very clearly understood; it can just happen—because of a compelling urge.

He has many friends, yet I always regard him as a lonely person. What he did only concerns himself, and the full consequences of his action are to be borne only by himself. He once said to me, 'I learn many things since I came here.' But we have to remember that learning does not necessarily mean accepting; yet I would add that through the years he has accepted far more than he has rejected.

I have often been aware that he is overtaxing himself, but he wants to dance, all the time, everywhere. 'The West' has got him by the throat, for we commercialise everything and everyone in our world theatre scene. There was an innocence about his dedication when he first came out of Russia that invested his performances with an unforgettable detachment and purity far removed from the screaming fanatics that surrounded him. But now he is their slave, and travels and dances where they bid. At moments one feels that the writing is on the wall, and he will have to learn to restrain his numerous performances. He has something of the spirit of Pavlova in him, though he belongs to today and not to yesterday. Pavlova was content to roam the world, well satisfied with a few classical ballets that suited her, and with the productions curtailed to fit the modest demands of her small company. But he wants to dance everything; whether he is first, second or third cast simply does not worry him, so long as he gets a performance of what is to him a 'new' choreographic experience. Perhaps this restless searching may one day result in some interesting choreographic works; his enquiring mind, with its limitless curiosity, must eventually have some other outlet.

His other gifts? Curiously linked to his passionate temperament is a pedagogue's mind, and therein lies—fallow for the moment—a possible great teacher for the future. No dancers working with him fail to give of their best, for he is a painstaking and very exacting instructor. He executes his exercises with deep concentration, and technical arguments fill him with interest—one senses a basis of knowledge that has been conscientiously acquired. What he may achieve in this direction one day—when his best dancing years are over—makes exciting and hopeful thinking.

With it all, he remains intensely Russian. The personality may be submerged, dedicated to the style of the ballet of the moment; the aesthetic appreciation unfolds—secretive and orderly; the mind is alerted, with all its acute sensitivity, to the choreographer's demands—but the nationality is there. Unasserted, unlabelled, it is something that you feel but may not at the time necessarily recognise for what it is, not for that matter always accept as actually befitting the occasion!

Famous today in the wide world of the dance, Rudolf Nureyev in his middle thirties has fifteen years of Western outlook stretching behind him. He is no longer a boy as he was when he arrived, but a man of solid artistic achievement, and he may well continue the pattern of his immediate yesterday through another decade. Time encircles him, always offering the opportunity to catch up with last week's achievement, or to improve on tonight's ('You should have come last night, I was better'); and he will continue to circle the world as an expression of his fierce fight for independence. Amidst the whirl of it all he will also continue to see every new play, film exhibition, opera and ballet he can squeeze into an overloaded time-schedule.

Sometimes I read stories of an arrogance of manner in public. I understand its possibility, particularly in the beginning when he must surely have felt a defensive necessity to take a definite line in public. But underneath it all I suspect that there was a mixture of suspicion and insecurity arising from his early experiences. He is undeniably temperamental—the intense vitality which can suddenly light up his dancing may break out in nervous irritation, even fury. But it is gone as quickly as it came. Such outbursts are almost always caused through a real anxiety about his work; nevertheless, this can often be an unfair strain on those in control.

I know no one who bestows praise with more generosity. ('The Royal Ballet is lucky to have *both* Dowell and Wall.') He is uninterested in the kind of gossip which circulates in ballet, inevitable in all tightly knit communities. Here I sense a singular sensitivity to being 'the stranger in our midst'. Our artists know him and understand him, as only artists can understand each other, and he has a sincere regard for our company—a regard that very often emerges as strongly expressed admiration. I think that he was as lucky to meet us as we were to meet him.

But essentially he remains, and probably will remain, an outsider in our community. He has his own creed. He will live by it and fulfil it in his own time in his own way. A Russian poet, Alexander Tvardovsky, writing of his own philosophy, seems to sum it up faithfully.

> 'Responsible
> for my own, my own concern in life is this:
> of that which I know better than all others
> I want to speak. And speak the way I want.'

Are not these the words that Nureyev dances?

CHOREOGRAPHY
(1973)

'A poem—let us be quite frank about the physical
facts of it—must have a beginning, a middle and an
end, otherwise it will not be a whole thing. It must
have rhythm, which means one group of inflections
not merely following but caused of another. Its
images, drawn from the world of time and space, must
develop its theme, or develop out of its theme, a certain order and a certain relationship: one image
begets another as surely as one day telleth another.
Moreover, the reader will not take in the whole of the
poem simultaneously: for him too it is a series of experiences. Whatever modern philosophy may do, the
poet cannot in fact discard sequence, cannot discard
cause and effect, cannot work to a continuous
present ...'

C. Day-Lewis: The Poetic Image

'It is an age of fragments. A few stanzas, a few pages,
a chapter here and there, the beginning of this novel,
the end of that, are equal to the best of any age or
author. But can we go to posterity with a sheaf of loose
pages, or ask the readers of these days, with the whole
of literature before them, to sift our enormous rubbish
heaps for our tiny pearls?'

Virginia Woolf

112

The situation in the choreographic field is strangely repetitive. I can remember the 1920s and the very early 1930s when the modern (now contemporary) dance was a rising force ... the lull came, and with it a reinforced 'establishment'.

Today we contend with a very much larger 'contemporary' swing in every direction of our living, our thinking and also our creative work in the theatre.

Gallantly the ballet joins in—and even *Swan Lake* has had, in one case, a Freudian look bestowed on her so far unruffled feathers (the Oedipus complex was found hard at work on the magician: 'he' became overnight a 'she'—and that 'she' was also 'The Queen Mother'—both roles played by the same artist with a change of costume but no change of make-up).

We know today that a great deal of traditional learning is regarded with a certain suspicion; everything and everyone is so speeded up that concentration and reflection are really very hard to come by.

We certainly do not want to return to the days of the donnish pedagogue—in any branch of learning—whose knowledge was as profound as the boredom that he could inflict on his listeners. But with all respect I do not think that the teacher's answer, in any field today, is as yet the right one; there is a sincere effort at work to solve the problem of pupil–teacher relationship, but the result is often just a matter of leaving the solution to the pupil or the student. Meanwhile the teacher persuades himself that this liberal-minded outlook is the answer. A well known actress told me, with gay nonchalance (and a well produced pre-war voice), how 'out' any dramatic studies were—and that 'we learn from our students today'. She was obviously in the middle of a difficult course of being 'with it' at any cost—particularly at the cost of a little cold-blooded reasoning.

It is understandable that the choreographic scene is confusing—for it is developing a tendency to live and experiment in a no-man's land between real 'choreography' and 'studies in composition', and these choreographic studies very often show a tendency to become as terse and as stationary as a gymnastic exercise. Interesting as some experiments both big and little prove to be, and equally exciting the choreographer's latent talent—we are near to building up a question mark about our direction.

It has been said that the greatest freedom springs from the greatest discipline, and the greater part of choreography today has no more discipline than the other arts, yet all are as promising as ever in potentially rich creativity. Obsessed, as they are, and all ages have been, with the very natural and healthy business of unlearning, they are showing a tendency to forget that there is first the business of learning.

If this present display of free will cannot lead to that most precious possession—a disciplined freedom—the situation is bound to deteriorate.

Moving from the general to the particular I would suggest that one of the most serious offences is the almost inevitable use of the record and tape-recorder for choreographic composition. The choreographer is consequently only alive to the general impact of sound; his work borders very closely on an 'improvisation', responding just to rhythm and certain well stressed accents and dynamics in the music.

Again I find that many young choreographers are no longer inclined to work in the theatre as dancers for the necessary length of time that would enable them to absorb, at close quarters, the craftsmanship of established choreographers. Many of them are missing those years of acquiring insight into the correct handling of their medium, the dancer, and do not experience the slow unfolding of enlightenment to be found in the shrewd touch of artistry that is to be studied at work in the final rehearsals on the stage.

These reflections remind me of a story of the early 1930s. A young, very young, choreographer, was working on the Sadler's Wells Ballet Company. His approach was stiff with the shortcomings that I have been dwelling on. A certain step, difficult to execute, and isolated completely from the possibility of fusion with the other movements, was causing tension. It was suddenly

114

executed with extreme exaggeration by a bored young male dancer. 'That's right,' exclaimed the excited choreographer, 'you've got it ...' and the young Walter Gore, still executing the step, danced towards me murmuring—'And now I've got it, what do I do with it?'

Rarely today is a choreographer commissioned to execute a specified choreographic work. He is his own master; he plays his own tune, or rather hunts for it in a discotheque. He seldom knows what it is to be confronted with a work that has an 'image' that he is asked to interpret creatively—a work already alive with an idea or a theme in its musical composition. This form of choreographic composition fills the younger generation with horror; they are not technically prepared or versed in the necessary disciplines and craftsmanship that can further interpret an image that exists, and exists with form and a sense of unity; they are not alive to something that needs a certain amount of objective handling.

Such demands are a challenge at any time, but today they are not understood—or perhaps not accepted, because any fundamental attitude that gives equality of thought to the relationship of the part to the whole has been partly obliterated, in a confused approach to any unity of thought in general. The subject matter of choreographic work is treated with indifference; they do not regard its development as a challenge to their creative sense—it can live or die on its own.

Yet I must emphasise again that the present young school of choreographers is rich in invention, skilled in the portrayal of movement for movement's sake. But they cannot escape the fact that there is yet a further reckoning. They will have to set their house in order and do with 'modern' ballet (in every sense of the word) what the Diaghilev choreographers did with the unharnessed technical virtuosity of the late nineteenth-century ballet.

Choreography should be rich today (and at times it is) with its two forms so fully developed along their respective lines of pedagogy; the sculptural quality of contemporary dance, with

115

an inspiration deeply embedded in Eastern movement, and the more sophisticated technique of the ballet springing from social and theatre development down through the centuries, with the roots in the dance movement, pattern and 'steps' of European folk and national dances; in the theatre the classical school has proved itself to be a great time-traveller as well as an interpreter of its own age.

Experiments today in both schools may well get out of control. Everything is subjected to the effort of an exaggerated highlighting of a special choreographic *movement* rather more than a *moment* in time; and this can bear a haphazard resemblance to a starving man searching for something to eat. Superficial philosophy may be lavishly laid out in the programme, though time and again it is not even superficially conveyed on the stage.

There seems to be a form of slickness at work that may in time undermine the prevalent widespread talent.

Could there be such a thing as 'choreographic' doodling? The thought came to me after watching three or four evenings devoted to experimental work—both classical and contemporary. How does one doodle? You start with a few lines and develop them (or rather they develop themselves) by idly permitting your pen to add to the extremities of the original lines.

Suddenly it all looks interesting, looks like a pattern. Do you go forward towards a climax? Oh no! You just extend the embryo pattern with your mind in a two-dimensional state until there is no more paper, and so it is finished without a finish. Sometimes there is too much paper, so you go on and on with your doodle until there is a tired looking fade-out. Either way the journey has no real significance.

Substitute in the above, the word 'paper' for 'music', and further recall earnest undergraduates overcome with inarticulation, stating on the television that 'you know what I mean ...' But we do not know most of the time.

Psychiatrists are interested in doodling, not for the artistry but as a means of studying the doodler's mind. Personality plays

116

its part in all art, but it is by no means the whole of the answer.

Where do we go from here with our talented younger school indulging in a tentative drop-out?

On the practical side it is possible that many dancing careers will be cut short through accident. These accidents may be the result of choreographers indulging in an unscientifically constructed movement for excitement's sake. These efforts do not represent 'choreography', they are rather more in the nature of freelance visual flights into the sensational, and at the expense of the performer.

A singer has his range; a musical instrumentalist has his; before it is too late choreographers must recognise that when it comes to the classical dancer he has his also, and to strain beyond this is to ask of him to become a skilful acrobat or gymnast—as well as a highly trained exponent of his own medium. This cannot be done. Life is not only too short, but any one form of perfected training in a highly specialised medium cancels out the full acceptance of other forms; too great a mixture results in muddled compromise that is of very little use to any whole.

There are, of course, certain fundamental scientific exercises, and for that matter movements, that are useful and interchangeable for classical ballet, contemporary ballet, acrobatics and gymnastics; but care should be taken not to confuse the issue, resulting in a choreographic demand that properly belongs to the circus or the gymnast.

At any time and in any country, where there is a temporary shortage of a requisite number of good choreographers, such an exaggeration in execution is to be noticed. The late nineteenth century saw the technique of the dance reach (choreographically) an ugly state of sheer virtuosity. It is the Soviet Union that has turned in the last thirty years (with a shortage of good choreographers in their Republics) to fantastic acrobatic feats—now laboriously copied by the West. A new choreographic work is sometimes alluded to by the critics as 'containing several Bolshoi lifts'. Unfortunately it all sounds, in the

117

reading, like the distribution of points between two football teams.

There must be an image; it is the spirit behind all choreography; and once projected, it is developed or replaced by another that shows some form of progress in time. There must be, even in the most abstract of ballets, a sense of harmony, a sense of relationship between one passage and another.

The critics are now beginning to show signs of weariness. In the past they have given earnest readings of their own as an explanation of obscure works. Time and again, when reading the reviews, it did not seem possible that they had all witnessed the same work, so different was the explanation of the possible basic theme. When we are confronted with a scenario of naïve pomposity, stiff with confused philosophy, do the critics ever say that the basic weakness of the whole project was its collection of rather painfully obvious impracticalities? I do not think that it is only a commendable wish not to discourage the choreographers, I often sense first night nerves on the part of the writers—paralysing any form of objective approach. This is surely understandable with Fleet Street on the doorstep demanding on one viewing and within the hour, what should in theory be a leisurely objective criticism of a complex choreographic work, a work that may have had many months of heavy labour bestowed on its birth.

I do not, though, want to confuse the obscurity of the unskilled and the temporarily muddled with that form of obscurity whose complexity holds a rewarding revelation that can be discerned deep and whole within itself, 'an image of mysterious wisdom won of toil' (Yeats). Concentration will bring this to light; it needs no explanatory shot in the dark from a member of the critic's circle that an inarticulate creative mind is content to accept the morning after as a possible explanation of his own original 'deep revelation'.

We all believe in today's young choreographic world; we could not do otherwise as we recall moments of real penetrating beauty, flashes of insight that could lead almost anywhere if

118

only they, the choreographers, would hold on to those principles that have actually put them where they are.

It is obvious that a creative freedom of approach must not be choked by 'establishment leadership'. If we let life get too dull we shall join that avalanche of dead-end opera houses tucked away in a state of stupefying security all over Europe.

When society itself is going through a process of confusion and change, choreographers, as other artists, become increasingly introspective. It is not just a matter of research for fresh inspiration, but often a form of escapism that leads to a disintegration of the relationship of the part to the whole. The search for imagery becomes more confused than inspired.

A worrying matter is the attitude of the modern choreographer to any reconstruction of his work; this remark, though, bears no relation to an artist's loss of interest in a work that never fulfilled his aim in any part of its composition.

A great deal of attention is given by choreographers to developing or expressing themselves through a restatement of the classics. But what about their own ballets? Here lies a sorry tale of neglect, and this weakness is universal.

A new English ballet is made and then displayed; it, generally speaking, continues as on the first night's presentation for ever and a day, or is hastily removed from the repertoire. Circumstances to a great extent have brought this about. The theatre, or theatres as the case may be, have little time to reconsider changes, nor is there ever enough time available for the first staging of a work.

A first night has become something of a hit or a miss. A full-length ballet is produced in England in a matter of three or four months (and I know of one that was mainly choreographed on an eight-week provincial tour); in the Soviet Union a ballet of such proportions would proceed at a leisurely pace. A British choreographer with many musical problems not yet resolved in a new work may find that the orchestra is pressing for the musical director's immediate attention, and asking for the rehearsal schedule in full by an early date. Consequently the necessary extra time schedules that should be available for musical readjustments are not by any means always forthcoming.

On the whole the choreographer is the one most at fault, for he has fallen into the habit of permitting his work to capitulate to the atmosphere created on the first night. Down through the years his approach to revision, even when it happens (and that is not often), is half-hearted; but in all fairness it must be borne in mind that the situation has deteriorated through the difficulties to be found time and again in the theatres, difficulties that are mainly due to their overloaded time-tables.

The critics do not always appear to understand the importance of their contributions to reconstruction. On an average they state their case more or less in full on one special viewing. Down comes the curtain and off to Fleet Street goes the review; it is a hideous and quite impossible task, a barbarous custom.

When will the pen be mightier than the pirouette? Soon, we hope.

But for many years now I have had little patience with the choreographers. Why are they so content to leave well (or ill) alone? Do they know how writers restate their case? The revision work done by composers? Choreographers appear to have developed through the savage speed, bustle and discomfort of creative work in our repertory companies, an attitude of finality to a 'first night', and they apply the same attitude to the morning reviewers of the work who time and again make mistakes in their own medium.

'Good' and 'bad' criticisms of a new work are—according to the skill with which they are written—either helpful or the reverse; but the first viewing is a first performance on the part of the critic, and his writings should be judged with reservation next day, both by himself and others. It is unwise for a choreographer to be unduly influenced by criticism good or bad, for he must learn to be his own severest critic. To admit that he knows certain passages are unsatisfactory, yet allow performances of the work to continue to be shown without imposing revision on every possible occasion, is to fail himself, his artists, his theatre and the critics.

My thoughts are occupied with this shortcoming through the contact I have had with it in the past. Always I found myself up against that fatalistic attitude towards what the critics had said and the immediate reaction of the public. I would like choreographers to try and see that these points, in the beginning, are only one part of the picture. The whole has had a great deal of thought bestowed on it, and the thought has next to be expressed in action; this may mean many a reassessment in the immediate future. In such cases courage and tenacity are not expressive of a lack of humility; on the contrary, the lack of them may suggest this very weakness.

The big repertory theatres need to allow space in their planning during a season—space that would not be concerned with a new production, but would be at the disposal of those works that hold a stable position in the repertoire in spite of some blatant shortcomings ... such a moment would permit everyone concerned to work on production points that require a restatement, particularly with regard to the lighting-plots, one of the most sorry time sufferers in the theatre.

The position of a ballet company is much more exacting than that of an opera. Everyone demands at least two or three new ballets every season, really 'new' ballets staged for the first time. This does not happen in the opera world. The opera classics come back time and again heavily decorated with visiting stars.

No ballet can be notated until it is composed—at least not at the moment as choreographers are not yet notators. This means that the initial composition is worked out on the dancers. A movement that lasts three minutes may take anything up to an hour before it is basically composed in a satisfactory way, and before any serious study and development can be achieved. I do not expect to live long enough to see choreographers notating their own initial composition scores. Once it was the order of things, and the reinstallation, I hope, is only a matter of time, thanks to the practicalities of the Benesh Notation. At the

121

moment we choreographers, to put it brutally, indulge in a form of improvisation, and leave the stabilising of our work to the dancers, notators and *répétiteurs*. It would be well if we were held responsible for the writing of our first rough score. If at any time there is the urge to arrange all the choreography on the dancer, the choreographer, knowing notation, would anyway be in a position to read the notator's recording, and to see if all that he finds stated therein is a true record of his composition.

It would be interesting to persuade the younger school of choreographers to take a new look at things. To say, 'I am not ready, and my ballet cannot go on.' I know of one promising short work lately produced, full of errors and damned by everyone but the writer, who strongly felt what time and revision could have done for it. One of its major setbacks during production was a continual change of cast in the leading role; three times was the dancer replaced during a very speedy rehearsal period. Remember, that as things are, a choreographer writes his ballet on his dancers; imagine the confusion if, during the initial creation of the role, the leading character in the ballet is subjected to three changes of cast in a very short period of time.

For the younger generation sometimes to work on the shortcomings of a promising but unfulfilled creation could be more profitable than a fresh start on a new work.

Certain remarks in the foregoing pages lead up to the various attitudes that are adopted towards what might be entitled The Petipa Poetic Licence.

It is wiser to accept the fact that 'Petipa choreography' in an unsullied form, may well no longer exist.

What does remain, and it is of immense importance, is 'Petipa style', but when the word 'remain' is used it must be understood that good examples of such pure classicism are few and far between.

The confusion started in Russia where we know that

122

Gorsky—one of Petipa's assistants—eventually choreographed for Moscow his own versions of the great Petipa ballets. Prior to this, we have Petipa's reaction to Gorsky's staging of several of the original Leningrad Petipa ballets in Moscow ...* 'had the impertinence to cripple them and lower them in the estimation of the public, by meaningless innovations and changes' ... and later, when in retirement, he states that his ballets were being given at almost every ballet performance in Leningrad, but he adds a complaint to the effect that they had 'not bothered to rehearse them'. One can imagine the result of such an attitude of indifference to his work, and the inevitable changes that must have gradually taken place later, in an effort to come to terms with the approaching choreographic changes towards the immediate past.

In our agitation to assess anything that is happening today in such a work as *Swan Lake* we are inclined to forget the general confusion that has been created in the past, a confusion not helped by the fact that two out of the four acts of the Leningrad production bear the master signature of Ivanov. If we except, for the moment, the famous *pas de deux* in Act III, and a few other classical numbers, surely the greatest classical moments are arrived at in the pure Ivanov classicism throughout Act II and Act IV? Again, we have to remember that the Bolshoi shows, in the Gorsky version, the influence of Ivanov in these two acts.

Petipa was essentially French, and what he brought to Russia cannot be underestimated. I speak of his choreographic 'essence' as an example, and I speak again of his marvellous shaping of a ballet and his cooperation with his composer. There is also, for further consideration, his brilliant and very Western-Europe *terre-à-terre* steps. Of course much was, even in his time, abused, particularly in relation to the music score. The composers of ballet music had endless restrictions imposed on them, and it was Diaghilev who eventually moved away from this weary domination of the choreography over the music

* See *The Memoirs of Marius Petipa* by Lilian Moore, Dance Books, London. *N. de V.*

score. This prevalent late nineteenth-century decadence in the ballet did not go unnoticed by the dancers of the twentieth century; everyone knows of the restlessness about the classical scene in the opening years of this century in Russia, and the unrest was strongly supported by Fokine and several very distinguished state dancers of the younger school.

It is, I am sure, quite impossible to know when Petipa's choreography received its first of many revaluations, we do not even know how much of the choreography he may himself have changed to suit various artists, or how much they eventually changed to suit themselves. We shall never know, with any certitude, and it has now become a situation that makes it rather impossible to be too dogmatic about the result that we see today.

When I wanted to produce the classics at Sadler's Wells Theatre in the early thirtes I obtained the services of Nicolai Sergueeff, the Maryinsky's former ballet master and notator. He was, at that time, an émigré in Paris where he lived, or rather starved, with his Stephanoff notation scores. It struck me that his valuable knowledge would help us to get somewhere near the original version.

But I had one big problem. In 1921 Diaghilev had presented *The Sleeping Beauty* at the Alhambra, and this particular production had also been revived for him by Sergueeff. Diaghilev, though, had lifted into this 'Petipa' work several musical numbers from *Casse-Noisette*. In the case of the Sugar Plum Fairy (overnight she became 'The Lilac Fairy') the choreography used was by Ivanov. Madame Nijinska gave an infinitely more interesting choreographic development of the famous 'finger variation'—danced in the prologue by one of the fairies. I had the honour to be taught this personally by Nijinska when I took her place in this dance, in an effort made to release her from some of her dancing roles. ('Do not just point, make a spiral movement with your whole arm.') Sergueeff, when working at Sadler's Wells, reverted to the original dance. But Diaghilev always preferred Nijinska's arrangement, and after I had left the company he asked me one day to come to the Coliseum to teach the more modern arrangement to Madame Legat, who had been dancing the early Petipa version.

Madame Nijinska also re-choreographed various Ivanov dances originally set to the music from *Casse-Noisette*; but none of these could be considered for our production at Sadler's Wells, as we already had Ivanov's *Casse-Noisette* in our repertoire!

There is the question of the wood scene variation for Aurora; over the years—Covent Garden's first production of this ballet to be precise—the music has been changed from what was used in both the Alhambra and Sadler's Wells earlier versions. Only the opening step today remains of the supposed once upon a time Petipa choreography. The first new Covent Garden choreographic version of this dance was by Frederick Ashton and the second one by Kenneth MacMillan. I would like to state here that I have distinct memories at the Alhambra (1921) of at least two of the ballerinas executing *fouettés* in the wood scene, to the exclusion of some of Petipa's choreography. Sergueeff most certainly never included them in any part of this scene in his production for us at Sadler's Wells. 'Florestan and His Two Sisters' also had many innovations introduced by Nijinska; these were the arrangements that I executed later with Nikitina and Lifar, in the condensed one-act version of the ballet entitled *Aurora's Wedding*. Further innovations of this same *pas de trois* took place later in the Diaghilev Company by Balanchine, and again in the 1946 Covent Garden production.

There is no reason to assume that all Petipa's prolific choreography was worthy of survival, or even to imagine, if such a thing had been the case, that dancers, choreographers and ballet masters would not have tampered with it drastically through the years of general change and upheaval that followed his death. Yet to this day the true Petipa style, and a certain though dwindling number of untouched choreographic examples still do exist. There is enough left for our inspiration, our understanding and our veneration—for Petipa represents a whole era of choreographic development. It will prove itself to be the means by which we will carry the creative element within the great classical tradition forward, for Petipa is *the* example of French classicism, just as Ivanov was once an inspired example of an unmistakable Russian form of the classical school. His death, some years before that of Petipa, was a bigger tragedy for the Russian classical scene than I think has ever been realised.

What exactly is the position of the great classical *traditional* ballets today, whether we speak of French, Russian or Danish school? How do they fit into the present scheme of things? I feel that there will be, eventually, entirely new productions everywhere, for in many ways the present neo-classical choreographers feel the pull of these works as part of their inspirational heritage, and regard the reproduction of this traditional style as a challenge. In my opinion it should be tampered with as little as possible, for they are an even greater challenge to the aspiring ballerinas and classical male dancers who measure their personal abilities in any direction by their approach to the original classical readings of such ballets; they are again an education in traditional 'style' and in period theatre production for every follower of the ballet from a student to a balletomane; they are also an all-important historical background for choreographers, designers and critics.

In spite of all innovations, there is no doubt that Diaghilev held on to the Petipa style and preserved the great master's *basic* traditions in his Alhambra production of 1921. It was fortunate for our future that England was the one country to have seen his version in its first full-length presentation; this influence has had far-reaching effects on the English scene and the result has been commented on time and again outside the country.

I will end with an apt quotation from Quiller Couch:

> 'To be classical is not to *copy* the classics: to be classical is to learn the intelligence of the classics and apply just *that* to their present world ...'

It is this challenge that the younger school of choreographers are up against today.

126

MOVEMENTS

On the surface of a swift-flowing stream the reflections of things near or far are always indistinct; even if the water is clear and has no foam, reflections in the constant stream of ripples, the restless kaleidoscope of water, are still uncertain, vague, incomprehensible.

Only when the water has flowed down river after river and reaches a broad, calm estuary or comes to rest in some backwater or a small, still lake—only then can we see in its mirror-like smoothness every leaf of a tree on the bank, every wisp of a cloud and the deep blue expanse of the sky.

It is the same with our lives. If so far we have been unable to see clearly or to reflect the eternal lineaments of truth, is it not because we too are still moving towards some end—because we are still alive?

'Reflections' from Alexander Solzhenitsyn's Stories and Prose Poems

I

Except during the formative years of a breakthrough by some new balletic venture, it always strikes me that the three basic elements in ballet do not possess an equality of development, interest and progress at one and the same time. I refer to school, execution and choreography. In a new venture there is a vacuum to be filled; it demands a unified interest in all three component parts on a basis of equality. Later it will be noticed that one of the triad will predominate, the one that will be influencing, at that moment, the ballet world at large.

At a risk of superficiality we will look briefly at the last eighty to one hundred years. At the end of the nineteenth century there was a strong accent on execution, and virtuosity came into its own as the predominating feature. The first forty years of this century saw the ascent of choreography and there was a very changed order of outlook. From the middle of the 1950s we experienced a big swing to the importance of 'school' development from every angle: aesthetic, scientific, psychological; pedagogy was scrutinised afresh and the mechanism of the human body in action reassessed, with much thought given to movement development from sources that lay far outside pure classicism. We are very nearly back to movement for movement's sake, and virtuosity linked to the hazard of the gymnasium. It may well result in an accent on execution and a display of technical virtuosity (in all its diverse forms) as the predominant force at work over the whole.

I cannot help feeling that if the present high, almost obsessive standard of execution continues, coupled with the effect that it is beginning to have on choreography, we may well have to accept a temporary return to what happened at the end of the nineteenth century lifted into the more ruthless and diverse demands of the twentieth century.

II

Many years ago the Royal Ballet decided to foster and encourage the beginnings of the Benesh Notation. Its future importance for us in those days was surely obvious, for here was an English form of dance notation that seemed to be what the world of ballet required to be developed and perfected. It now appears to be accepted in the ballet profession as the most practical form of notation for the recording of repertory ballets.

The ballet world in general has been far too long solving the problem of a practical script that could prove to be as concise

(Above): John Cranko
'His reconstruction of the Stuttgart
Ballet will be a part of history in
the European ballet scene.' (Photo:
Robert Belton)

(Below): Kenneth MacMillan
'His major works are on the grand
scale, and that is rare today.'
(Photo: Anthony Crickmay)

(Above): Rudolf Nureyev
'There was an innocence about his
dedication when he first came out
of Russia.' (Photo: Anthony
Crickmay)

(Below): Monica Mason and
Anthony Dowell in *Song of the Earth*.
(Photo: Leslie E. Spatt)

(Left): Stephen Jefferies in *The Prodigal Son*. (Photo: Anthony Crickmay)

(Below): Margaret Barbieri and Alain Dubreuil in Peter Wright's production of *Giselle*. (Photo: Anthony Crickmay)

Margot Fonteyn, Michael Somes, Alexander Grant and the *corps de ballet* in the finale from Act I of *Ondine*, Ashton's last full-length ballet. (Photo: Roger Wood)

(Above): Antoinette Sibley and
Anthony Dowell in Kenneth
MacMillan's *Pavane*. (Photo: Jennie
Walton)

(Below): Lynn Seymour and
Anthony Dowell in *A Month in the
Country*. (Photo: Anthony
Crickmay)

(Above): Wayne Sleep as 'Hop o' my Thumb' in *The Sleeping Beauty*. (Photo: Anthony Crickmay)

(Below): Michael Coleman in *La Fille Mal Gardée*. (Photo: Leslie E. Spatt)

Symphonic Variations
(Above): Moira Shearer, Michael Somes, Pamela
May and Margot Fonteyn (1946). (Photo: Baron)
(Below): Laura Connor, David Wall, Jennifer
Penney and Merle Park (1973). (Photo: Anthony
Crickmay)

To Madam
With my greatest admiration
and fondest love
Alexander

'When we were very young.'
(Above): Alexander Grant, aged
five.
(Below): Lesley Collier
(foreground) at White Lodge, aged
twelve.

for the dancer as the music score is for the musician. We have, in the past, placed ourselves in a position which led to choreography being accepted in the eyes of the world as a form of improvisation. Of course, the problem has had the full and able attention of many distinguished former notators in the history of the ballet. All the various systems through the centuries have been of extreme importance, and have added to the enrichment of the dance history scene. Notably in modern times there is Labanotation (1925) which is still used today by the greater number of contemporary (modern) dance groups. But the classical ballet, because of its ever expanding position in the theatre for over three hundred years, has always proved to be the biggest problem, and Rudolph Benesh realised the importance of the whole issue when he set about studying our requirements.

There still persists the idea, and strangely enough among dancers and *répétiteurs*, that 'film is the answer'. The film is, of course, an admirable means of recording a ballet and it is practical to use it in certain cases—such as close-up study of an artist's particular *interpretation* of a role—or to give a general *visual* survey of one particular production. But in its essence a film is the same thing as the recorded playing of a musical composition, just as the spoken word in play or film or on the radio is only a recorded playing of an actor's interpretation of the writer's script.

The work of a choreologist (or notator) is not to be confused with the important work of the choreographer and his two principal assistants— the *répétiteur* and the ballet master—in any production of a ballet. Notation is essentially basic; it is a record of the choreographer's own work and its relationship to the music; it is the only fundamental evidence for posterity of the original choreographic script, but it must not be assumed that it is necessarily concerned with interpretation and production.

I would say that it is becoming increasingly important that the notating of a ballet must be undertaken during the *original* production rehearsals. One hears about discrepancies creeping

129

into a notation score, and this has very often proved to be a legitimate complaint. Yet time and again this is due to the notator, at a later date, adding some missing movements (or whole dance sequences) given by a dancer whose choreographic interpretation has strayed from the choreographer's original conception.

In the future, students in the Royal Ballet School will be expected, when they enter the company, to be able to read notation with ease. We visualise a day when a young artist will be capable of putting in some private study, through notation reading, of the many roles to be learnt in a big repertory company.

It should be appreciated that to become a good notator means that there must be present a certain talent as specific and highly specialised as that which is found in a good teacher, *répétiteur*, or choreographer. They, like other specialists, are born not made; it is proving to be an interesting branch of the staff work with many possibilities for those who (a) show a preference for it from the very beginning as a full-time career, or (b) are interested in the prospect of taking it up in the latter part of their work in the theatre.

In time there will be a less sharp division between notators, ballet masters and *répétiteurs*, and that day will be when notation has become an everyday subject in the dancer's training years. It is clear that everyone learns to read and write, and a dancer must eventually be able to read movement as the basis of his general dance education, having in the first place submitted to the necessary amount of dance notation study.

It should be emphasised that because the Benesh Notation has served the repertory ballet companies so well it is not to be assumed that there are not other significant fields for its use. In Italy it has been taught to the staff for some years in the physiotherapy department of a hospital for spastic children, and the recording in detail of these children's movements has led to some interesting observations, and opened up a way to a new form of study for the physiotherapists.

A night in February 1973 found me as usual at the Albert Hall
Folk Dance Festival. The occasion had a very special significance: for the first time some thirty to forty students of the
Royal Ballet Junior School (aged eleven to sixteen) were taking
an important part in the evening's entertainment; they had
appeared before on a modest scale, but on this particular night
they had sufficient dances to execute to entitle them to be listed
among the major contributors.

The Albert Hall Folk Dance Festival has its own rarified
atmosphere with an audience (alas!) very far removed from the
spectators who fill the Royal Opera House. I did not spot one
ballet critic. Of course, I may be in error—there was, after all,
an audience of many thousands. The great Victorian hall seems
perfectly suited for the casual comings and goings of those vast
crowds. The atmosphere is never charged with any visible
effort, nor does it ever show tension on the part of either
audience or performer. All day long the groups arrive from
every corner of the British Isles; it is half the charm, of course,
that it should appear as lacking in any feeling of hurry as a
holiday in Ireland. There is the same unhurried approach to
be noted even among the most virile of the highly skilled foreign
guest performers. The foreign contribution is always immensely
rewarding, and it should be noted that the visitors' brilliantly
executed dances do not ruin 'the message', but only underline
its significance.

With the enthusiastic help and intelligent understanding of
the Royal Ballet School's present teachers of Folk Dance studies
at White Lodge, Ronald Smedley and Robert Parker, and the
support given to them by the Director Michael Wood and Ballet Principal Barbara Fewston, we were on this occasion wit-
nessing a breakdown of that former prejudice in England,
namely the dislike of the thought of any professional approach
towards our country's dances. On this occasion the Folk Dance
audience left us in no doubt—it was a wildly enthusiastic recep-

tion that they bestowed on these young people, who were, with the background of their own disciplined technique, adding something of extra value and point to these dances that they were executing purely for the joy of dancing.

More and more are the youngsters at the Royal Ballet School asked to perform and show their skill in this direction; the prejudice is now also becoming a thing of the past among the students themselves, and this took some time to eliminate. Now they realise that they have positive proof that their labours are not in vain ... they may learn the Cumberland Reel early on in their school years, but they will recognise its influence in the finale of *La Fille Mal Gardée*. In this famous ballet of Frederick Ashton one can glimpse the skilled use and development that he has also made of sword dance routines, and there is an authentic Maypole Dance in the fête scene.

All through my career I have loved any form of national dance and Folk Dance figuration. I can recall, at a time when I seemed fated to dance every pizzicato in the Diaghilev repertoire, my joy when I was suddenly put into the Mazurka in *Swan Lake*. Out of the eight dancers involved four of them were Polish artists. I remember the Russians concerned, telling me to watch the Poles—'Only a Pole can really dance a Mazurka.' How right this advice was, and how aware I became of the feeling of fantastic exhilaration that their subtle rhythm conveyed. Again, when I watch the Georgian Dancers, and see a stream of elegant women executing beautiful hand movements, my mind travels back to a class at the Bolshoi when I witnessed these very hand movements given at the end of a class as an exercise.

If the Russians can develop the beauty and the breadth of these plastique movements that spring from the depths of their own soil we, in the West, may also preserve our own inheritance of speed, lightness, and neat footwork.

In the arts we will always whirl about in a devastating but courageous state of revolutionary restlessness, and it is not the concern of any of us to see our era in perspective, that is for those who eventually see it all from a comfortable distance. The view from the middle of the dress circle is more in focus than that from the front row of the stalls.

'Such stuff as dreams are made of' may rather depend on the stuff, for that happens to be the substance of the dream. The word 'dream' is complex, and would that the dreamer might know more about the matter; and so many of us remain thoughtful about the word 'stuff' in relation to many so-called dreams and their eventual forms.

Dance artists of this country are no longer in a dream world. The task ahead may prove to be harder than the one that has preceded it, for the pangs of birth, however painful, have a strong element of expectation about them. In the future smooth-flowing continuity is not to be expected, and a shrewd foresight is something that must be alerted. Even if the foresight sees moments that would appear to be negative there is a hidden strength in the capacity to sense adversity, to accept it, and to be able to set about procuring the 'stuff' of those dreams that can come to terms with it.

We must remember what has been done in this small country of ours. By far the most backward country in the world of ballet fifty years ago it has, in the face of things, made more than just progress. It has stabilised itself, and is now one of the cornerstones of the British theatre scene.

IMPRESSIONS

A VISIT TO RUSSIA: 1957

An overcrowded drawer of papers long forgotten; in it I find an exercise book, dated March–April 1957. I have left this diary as it was written during my second visit to Moscow twenty years ago. I went there six months after the proposed visit of the Royal Ballet to Russia in 1956 had been cancelled owing to the Hungarian uprising. I was there to partake in future arrangements for both the Russian companies and our own and to spend as much time as possible with the Moscow and Leningrad ballet schools.

I have slightly developed certain impressions, but only as I remember them racing through my mind at the time; I was too occupied to state, in more detail, all my reactions.

I have not otherwise tampered with this record; I do not want to kill any spontaneity that it may possess.

THE DIARY

MOSCOW

(Snow in early spring)

Through the double glaze of window panes I see
A whiteness that petrifies the city's life.
A driver with his horse and open cart awaits
The woman who stands alone, armed with a spade.
Partner she seems in a mighty perennial birth
That asks of her warm bloodstream aid to its toil.
Contention is the womb from which her aim
Leaps with a rhythm that bears the beat of spring
As high is flung the spade's unblemished load
Destined to fall within the waiting cart,
Where bitter bright appears the crystal spread.
The stretch of sack that covers all is drab
With dirt that stains the snow a muted brown.
On this rough bed she lies,
Staunch symbol of the land from which she springs.

N. de Valois

Tuesday 24th March, 1957
The first day amounts to waiting for someone to let me know
something about my schedule ... but there is always the view
of the Kremlin from my bedroom window in the British
Embassy. This Embassy is a comfortable, solid nineteenth-cen-

138

tury house once owned by the two Moscow 'sugar kings', whose collection of French Impressionists are now the pride of the Pushkin Museum.

I lunched with the British minister and his wife, and I gleaned that I would be taken by the Russians to see *The Three Sisters* that evening.

But I did not see them! When my interpreter arrived she informed me that the play had been cancelled; so instead I went to the Stanislavsky Theatre to sit through the embarrassments of Offenbach's *La Belle Hélène*. The voices were good and so was the burlesque acting. But there was an overall ugliness, not even highlighted—just flat and unrelieved.

The Stanislavsky audience seems to be poorer than the Bolshoi—there is an air of heavy provinciality that has died out of our own provincial theatres years ago ...

A form of Moscow depression descended on me; everything wore the repetitive spread of wet paint.

My interpreter is nice and very good-looking. She wears her simple clothes with dignity, and has no trace of powder or paint on her charming little face. Her command of English is not extensive but as far as it goes she speaks good English. Of course (as usual) she knows nothing about the ballet. She has been chosen from the 'pool' and is, I suppose, deemed to be a safe choice as her personal interests are directed towards literature and the drama.

She expressed some strong views on the Stratford Company; did not like Michael Redgrave's Hamlet, 'It was not Shakespeare ...' loved Dorothy Tutin. They preferred the Scofield Company (an independent venture that played there some years ago). Peter Brook was the producer—a Russian by birth.

Wednesday 25th March
I was at the Bolshoi by midday to see *Le Lac des Cygnes*. Cast: Odette-Odile, Christova; Prince, Zhdanov; Jester, Khomyakov; *pas de trois*, Gottlieb, Korataeva, Nikitin.

I have not been able to change my mind, I do not like this

production. There is a great deal of padding and indifferent execution. The *corps de ballet* in the swan scenes give by far the best dancing to be seen; in the last act not only were the dancers excellent, but the choreography on Gorsky's part was good. This is the only act wherein I like his version and this act shows some very definite Ivanov influences—more in style and approach than actual choreography.

Christova pleasing and beautifully made. To be frank, she does not compare favourably with any of her young British contemporaries. Not that such a comparison is easy, for there are many technically difficult steps omitted. I therefore could not judge how strong she may be, or perhaps hopes to be one day. Her Act III was overplayed. The Prince proved to be by no means a young man. He looked very plump in his heeled shoes and lavishly spangled tunic. As dressed for the ballroom scene I do not think that he could be presented anywhere outside Russia—where such costumes are still acceptable to both critics and public, and, we suppose, to the artists. (The poor man had to disport a tall aigrette fixed to the middle of the bandeau encircling his wig.)

The little Khomyakov (Jester) was very heavily built. But he danced brilliantly and cleanly—although in years well past his prime. Nikitin in the *pas de trois* was good; he has everything—good looks, good figure, good beats and elevation. He is quite a young man to watch . . .

Again, I could not judge the two girls Korataeva and Gottlieb. The choreography of their respective variations was simple to execute in comparison with the Petipa versions. The clearcut, intricate precision of the original choreography was lost; with the movements blurred, and the steps executed at half time, they appeared to dance 'through' the music rather than with it. Some pretty moments of musical phrasing, but the approach was alien to the ballet's original fundamental style and content.

Lovely as the Russian plastique work can be, and undeniably their major contribution to the modern classical school, this style is a follow-through of Fokine's style and the influence of the romantic school on him (*not* the influence of Isadora Duncan!) leading up to his own choreographic evolution. It is unnecessary, though, to inflict it on the original works of Petipa to the extent that they have done.

The national dances interested me. I first executed them myself with the Diaghilev Company and later saw the self-same dances passed on to our Company in the 1930s by Sergueeff, with the same approach and execution as with the Diaghilev version.

In Russia today these dances in the ballroom scene have greatly changed—they look artificial, affected. The Petipa dances were stately, yet executed with simplicity. The same thing has happened with the Spanish dance. Petipa's dignified dance has been turned into the frolics of four bashing, smashing Spanish gypsies. They execute it beautifully and it is exciting—but it is at loggerheads with the music, and no longer a pastiche of Spanish classical style.

After the depressing effect of the Stanislavsky's public on Tuesday night, the many enchanting children in the audience at the Bolshoi made a pleasant change . . . big parties of Indian, Chinese and Korean students were also everywhere.

Back to the Stanislavsky in the evening to see *Jeanne d'Arc*. I was deeply impressed. Allowing for a lack of period style, it is a work of imagination and power in spite of poor scenery and costumes. Bourmeister the choreographer has achieved, in places, the impossible. As an example, he has managed to present Jeanne as a classical dancer, despite her male clothing. The choreography (with certain lapses) was the richest and most varied that I have so far seen; the stage effects were, as usual, magnificent. Satisfying score.

Vlassova as Jeanne is, for me, the greatest little actress their ballet world possesses. She reaches extraordinary heights in this performance; I find her intelligence, style and general approach shows something of Western Europe's conception of Russian ballet at its best.

I met Bourmeister afterwards. He is an aesthetic both in appearance and conversation. I wondered if he had, with that name, a German ancestry; his face has nothing in common with his present compatriots. A very sad expression; although sensitive and intelligent, it is a humourless face, and Russian humour is as discernible as the Irish equivalent.

Thursday 26th March
This morning I see the fifteen- to sixteen-year-old girls in the seventh grade class under Madame Kozhukhova; she is about sixty-five but looks older, and is obviously ill. She told me that she had been to hospital three times with pneumonia.

The class was not very promising; out of fifteen or sixteen in number I saw only two of any real merit. All suffered from weak feet and elementary faults. All of them, though, had beautiful straight backs and good extensions. The actual class lesson was very good—but the careless execution was detrimental to what the lesson was trying to achieve.

After lunch I went to visit the boys' graduation class—eighteen years of age. Messerer was teaching, what a magnificent teacher! On the whole the talent was not very marked, except in two tiny boys (both Albanians). They were very small—about five foot six inches. They were marvellous, but looked like undersized footballers. One appeared to have a shin bone about four inches in length. Of course, in such cases of exaggerated points in the physical make-up, there is always the possible compensation of spectacular virtuosity in terms of elevation, *pirouettes* and '*batterie*'.

I next spent nearly two hours at the Pushkin Museum. I had only time today to see the famous French Impressionists collection. Such magnificent Gauguins, Renoirs and Matisses that were once mainly private collections ... as soon as I have a moment I must get back to this museum again.

A standing cocktail party at the British Embassy started at six fifteen p.m. and went on until nine o'clock. Met many Russians—also a great number of American and British.

142

The Bolshoi director was there, and with a certain pompous charm he told me of the 'virtues' of Russian ballet and the 'modern importance' of their present creative work. He spoke of Diaghilev and Fokine as if these two were an unknown quantity to me. An Embassy secretary interpreted for me and, noting the turn that the conversation was taking, told the director that I had been with the Diaghilev Company. I told him that we had both *Petrushka* and *Firebird* in our London repertoire, and gazing past me he murmured gently, 'Both those ballets are by Fokine you know ...' A kindly but condescending tone accompanied this enlightening statement. I then told him that I had danced in nearly the whole Fokine repertoire some forty years ago; he looked as if he did not know whether to accept the statement or blame the Embassy champagne.

He was nice though ... there just did not happen to be anything for him but Russia, Russian ballet and possibly Russian vodka.

Dined alone with the Ambassador, his sister and brother-in-law. A pleasant, quiet evening.

27th March (Good Friday)
Once more to Madame Kozhukhova's class—this time to see her sixteen- and seventeen-year-old girls. No outstanding talent with the exception of one girl who had, however, rather weak feet. It was a beautiful lesson, executed with good style and sense of movement; but certain basic faults were still to be seen here as elsewhere.

Midday found me at a Bolshoi matinée and my first glimpse of Plisetskaya ... She was quite lovely; a hard dancer one might say, but compensation lay in her lightness, and scintillating technique. A fine actress, and above the usual height of a ballerina. In this particular ballet she reminded me, in some obscure way, of Pavlova; she had something of Pavlova's cast of features and glowing magnetism. Never have I heard such an ovation for a dancer anywhere—they just worship her.

Laurencia does not make the same impact on this, my second,

143

viewing. The dances are exciting, but not really difficult to execute and the technical stunts (that left me breathless on my first visit) now wear an air of familiarity ... we must have made great technical strides in three years!

Tonight I attended—at the invitation of Zhukov of the Ministry of Culture—the dinner given in honour of the delegation that I came out with, but to which I am not really attached. Many speeches were made as we ploughed through the now all too familiar official dinner (hot-cold-hot-cold it goes, about three times round). The speeches were made by Mr Mayhew (our M.P.), Zhukov, Fitzroy MacLean and others.

The distinguished Russian poet Samuel Marshak was there. He also translates Burns and Shakespeare. We had a long talk; he told me, when he heard I was Irish, that he had translated W. B. Yeats (who is popular over here). He added that he had once met him. When I told him how well I had known the Irish poet he was deeply interested, and asked me a lot more about my past theatre ventures outside the more conventional ballet scene. I liked very much Solodovnikov, the director of the Moscow Arts Theatre. I have an open invitation to go to any of the performances. I sat next to Bogatyrev, the London Embassy Cultural attaché. At one difficult moment he was really very funny. When the Vice-Chancellor of Birmingham University mentioned Australia it created an awkward moment, for since the spying incident the Russians are not, as yet, diplomatically represented at Canberra. Bogatyrev, sensing my agitation, looked at me slyly and in a gravely Dublinish way he said, 'In Australia there are many kangaroos, all sorts of kangaroos—far too many kangaroos ...'

Russians have the Irish gift of slipping about like well greased eels—tweaking the tails of their opponents.

Saturday 28th March
To the Bolshoi in the morning to see the Bolshoi ballet classes. Madame Petrovna took the first. On account of a rehearsal call it was a mixed class of men and women. I was seeing an essenti-

ally routine class for the less talented, indeed most of the dancers belonged to the larger section of the *corps de ballet* who appear only in ballets and *divertissements* requiring a very large number of dancers.

The class that followed was taken by my beloved Messerer. This was properly controlled and all the best dancers were present. Ulanova, Plisetskaya and Christova were all there. Plisetskaya (Messerer's niece, by the way) was lovely to watch. I talked to her afterwards. I found her very sympathetic. I hope to see her rehearse *Le Lac des Cygnes* as I have to leave for Leningrad before the performance.

In the evening I spent three hours in the pretty little theatre affiliated to the Bolshoi watching an embarrassing production of *Coppélia*. It was danced by the not so prominent members of the Bolshoi. It was difficult for me to be impressed as before leaving London I had seen the Royal Ballet School's exciting first matinée performance of this work. These Bolshoi dancers were further hampered by poor choreography. As usual though, whatever the circumstances, you see one or two outstanding performances, in this case Dr Coppélius and Franz. Dr Coppélius was brilliant—a wonderful mimetic artist.

29th March (Easter Sunday)

The Easter service was held in a large downstairs hall in the Embassy. It was attended by our Embassy staff, the American staff and all the English families living in Moscow; afterwards the Ambassador departed—with his brother and sister-in-law—into the country to stay there until Monday night.

Here I am alone in the Embassy for forty-eight hours! Rather fun. There is hardly any staff. The chef has given me the run of his pantry for getting tea and light meals, as most of the kitchen staff have the day off, but he also left me a delectable cold meal in my room.

Again I feel a thrill of excitement from this unusual experience of finding myself, for once in a lifetime, in our Moscow Embassy all alone during an Easter weekend.

By midday I was back at the Bolshoi revelling in *The Fountain of Bakhchisarai*—a lovely barbaric work smelling of the East. Wonderful character dancing and a moving story from a Pushkin poem. I feel that it would lose a great deal removed from its own country. The staging would be extremely difficult to reproduce—and the atmosphere quite impossible to attempt to transfer. I was lucky to see it from the director's box with all its obvious advantages, and loved every minute of the performance.

In the evening I attended an opera performance. It was *A Life for the Tsar*—uneven; yet some good singing and the added interest of the famous Glinka ballet in the ballroom scene. The opening Polonaise in this ballet is marvellously presented. Men and women of all ages perform; they are all individual characters, made-up well and wonderfully characterised. The Russians are absolute masters of such a school of realism.

Again I sat in the director's box and was joined by the conductor in the intervals. He told me how he had prepared all our ballets—*Daphnis and Chloë*, and 'the wonderful *Firebird*'. Poor man! He said that he had had twenty rehearsal calls— (I doubt if we get that in a season).

30th March (Easter Monday)
Started a migraine this morning with a nagging headache. There were no rehearsals or classes scheduled for me, so I went back to the Pushkin Museum to see the rest of the paintings.

I returned to the Embassy for a cold lunch and then was taken once more to the Kremlin Churches (more wonderful than ever on a second visit). From there on to the University, which resembles an enormous Lyons Corner House. I was taken over it by a boy student who spoke good English. He was as enthusiastic as he was earnest and unconsciously funny. He knew (a) the cubic measurements of the students' private sitting-room; (b) the cubic measurements and number of big halls that held 2,000, 1,000 and 700 students respectively and (c) the number of small halls holding 500 and 250 ... He was inordinately proud of 'foreign country students'. 'We have,' he said, as we swept panting down a long corridor, 'just passed an American student. We have,' he said, increasing his speed, 'a drama club, an opera club. We produce dramatic plays and operas and we give concerts. Someone has said that some of our drama students are as good as professionals.' I told him that many a great English actor had sprung from a university dramatic club. He didn't appear to be interested; I don't think that he thought any allusion to the English could be interesting in any sense, or bear any relation to the present conversation, which he was anyway bent on making as epigrammatic as possible.

I witnessed some intriguing gymnastics and swimming and also saw a Chinese play in progress in a very nice theatre.

After two hours the migraine had taken over from everything ... I had to cancel *Le Lac des Cygnes* at the Stanislavsky and retire to bed.

Tuesday 31st March

To a routine Bolshoi company class at the theatre (Petrovna) and on to an interesting rehearsal of their American concert programme.

Some good character numbers but not very good classical arrangements. The latter were either wildly acrobatic or equally wildly dull—except for some of Jacobson's short numbers. Ulanova sat in front of me but had little or nothing to say. She would not rehearse as she was not feeling well.

The migraine won again; the effort of coming out had made it much worse. I returned to the Embassy and submitted to an injection given to me by the Embassy doctor. I was sad, though, to cancel out an opera performance that night.

Wednesday 1st April

Today was been extremely cold. I saw a very interesting children's class (twelve and thirteen years of age) under a good woman teacher. She was excellent in theory, but somehow failed to stop things taking a wrong turning in practice. The children were enchanting with their grace and ease of manner. Their deportment their strongest point (as usual)—foot work as unstable as ever. I had a long talk with the teacher afterwards and was able to clear up some technical differences that were puzzling me. I also obtained from her an interesting exercise for first and second-year children who are stiff in the hip joints.

This evening I went to *The Queen of Spades*. Very enjoyable. On the whole the production was on a higher level than the singing. The Countess, though, was a fine singer and a wonderful actress.

Thursday 2nd April
The day of the state examination of the top class students. Nine girls and ten boys passing out. The entire staff of both company and school were present. The atmosphere was exhilarating—and the examiners kind and sympathetic; I could use the word 'devoted', because there is ever present here a devotion of the teacher to the pupil. The boys were far ahead of the girls on this particular occasion. I found the girls' work rather a 'bluff' for a passing out examination. Their class was arranged and taken by Smirnova. It was carefully planned to show them to every advantage. Very 'pretty' with some lovely adagios, good steps of elevation, but *petite batterie* non-existent. No hard routine *barre* exercises; it was all in the form of a dance arrangement—skilfully and tastefully thought out ...

Not so with the boys! Messerer's own top class, and he took it himself. These boy students were wonderful. With a broad smile of complete confidence their teacher showed an approach that was professional and devoid of any form of lip service. Every academic technical step was executed. I could grasp the extent of their strength and weakness, and the strength far surpassed any weakness. The audience expressed their approval with applause and 'bravos'; there had been rather a quiet reception for the girls ...

It appears that the examining board had a great argument afterwards. Madame Kozhukhova stood firm—she was furious with the others for accepting any of the girls. She said that to allow them to continue was 'to ruin their lives meant to be lived in a more ordinary occupation'. She said to send them to the opera houses elsewhere in the Soviet Union was 'to show the Republics what bad dancers were coming out of the Bolshoi School'. (There was just one girl, though, who was very talented; but she was tall, and no doubt Madam would not accept her height at any cost!)

Of course I am only repeating what was told to me; as an outsider I was not present when the staff discussed the examination. But it all had for me a slightly familiar ring about it; these arguments and troubles are to be found in every state ballet company and school.

The afternoon found me, with one of our Embassy's secretaries, sitting round a table with members of 'The Cultural Relations Groups for All Countries'. I found myself speaking slowly and answering questions almost in words of one syllable. When we came to 'abstract painting' it was hard going—they tended to develop a positive enmity towards the subject.

Natalia Roslavleva was present and was a tower of strength and understanding. She held the reins firmly. She is an exceedingly intelligent woman and was, on this occasion, bent on exacting an unimpeded approach from everyone.

In the evening I went to see *Cinderella* at the Bolshoi. I now see all the ballets from the director's box which I like very much; although close to the stage it has a perfect view of every scene in full. I was, choreographically, bitterly disappointed. There is no point in analysing this production; my disappointments are too numerous, and worse, my familiarity with the score (in my opinion superior to *Romeo and Juliet*) did not help to soften my disillusion.

Friday 3rd April
More classes in the morning ... then the dress rehearsal for America's 'Recital Programme'.

It was just like all such affairs; arguments with the conductor over tempi, but the dancers were infinitely more demanding

149

:ct than their contemporaries would dare to be in
nnumerable good, bad and indifferent dancers.
ers, though, were superb.

ng Beauty pas de deux was rearranged, simplified and
ruined. The Blue Bird suffered the same fate; it was about half
as difficult as the original Petipa choreography.

Ulanova danced two numbers with a breath-taking purity
of line. For the rest, some of the dances showed the younger
dancers to advantage, but the arrangements in general were
not interesting.

One young choreographer had choreographed three variations inspired by three Rodin statues in one of their museums.
They were pleasant studies in a modern vein. The Bolshoi
Faculty was shocked and deemed them 'too erotic' ... I had
a talk with Messerer who was both puzzled and depressed. He
said he had hoped that the Bolshoi Ballet would be able to steer
clear of these influences ... he added (a) that you need not study
ten years to execute this sort of dancing—three years would be
enough; (b) he found it vulgar . . .

Saturday 4th April
Went to the nine a.m. class at the Bolshoi under Madame
Gerdt. A beautiful and dignified woman; a product of the Leningrad of pre-revolutionary days. Speaks French perfectly.
They are, all of them, obviously as much in awe of her as they
are of her teaching. To my delight it reminded me in principle
so very much of the present-day English School. She told me
that she had also been a pupil of Cecchetti. She asked to be
remembered to Karsavina and Lopokova. She added that she
was in the command performance that the Russian Ballet gave
at Covent Garden for the Coronation of King George V in 1911.
I found her nostalgic memories of the Covent Garden Opera
House very touching, 'and the market,' she added, 'the
romantic market . . .' It was rumoured that she had requested
(and had had her request accepted) that she should teach exclu-
sively the same class up through the school for a number of

years—she did not wish to have a change of pupils. I think that she sensed, or rather knew, that her schooling—in comparison with the modern Russian School—amounted to a traditional system of its own.

I have only been able to pack and write letters since lunch, and give my radio talk which the Russians will broadcast to England on their own radio next Tuesday ...

My train leaves about eleven p.m. and gets into Leningrad at eight a.m. Monday morning.

Sunday 5th April
The journey to Leningrad was rather strange. On boarding the train I found myself in a four-berth carriage with two other women and one man ... The latter went down to the toilet to prepare for bed, and came back clothed in his pyjamas—but they were not graced by a dressing-gown. I just lay down with my dressing-gown over my dress, but my female companions had meanwhile disrobed. No one thought anything about this mixed bathing. Our male companion was very nice and polite and totally at ease with us all. The train ran smoothly and the berth was comfortable. I slept better than I generally do on such train journeys ...

Leningrad is beautiful; the Palace square with the Hermitage on one side is a wonderful sight—and the great sweep of seventeenth-century houses lifted me right out of myself and the heavy schedule of programmes arranged.

Within three hours I was sitting in the director's box at the Kirov Theatre, once the famous Maryinsky. It is a dream in gold and blue—not by any means as big as the Bolshoi, but with far more emphasis on period and dignity ...

I saw *The Stone Flower*. A good ballet, and so much more in keeping classically with our own form of choreography and production in the West. Three fine young dancers danced the leading roles.

Everyone was relaxed and friendly. I had a long and pleasant chat in the interval with the director. I asked to meet the three

151

young principal artists, and without any fuss I was brought onto the stage through the pass door after the performance to chat with them. They were very friendly and natural.

I left the theatre feeling that I was only a stone's throw away from Covent Garden Opera House . . .

In the evening I went to the Maly Theatre. Another enchanting old theatre, but small. It houses opera and ballet—a Leningrad Sadler's Wells. I saw a Strauss ballet entitled *The Blue Danube*. The dancers were good, the choreography adequate for the style of the ballet which is frankly sentimental—a *Lilac Time* period ballet. The leading ballerinas are both good dancers—with certain reservations that are not in any way connected with their actual technical performances.

Monday 6th April

A pleasant day. It was the theatre's 'free day' so I was at liberty to spend all my time sight-seeing.

First I was driven round this wonderful city with its seventeenth and eighteenth-century squares, palaces and streets— (one nostalgic moment made me feel that Dublin was Leningrad's very small and very poor relation!) I saw Kschessinska's palace and thought of the little old lady that I had last seen in Paris when we went on our E.N.S.A. tour in 1945. I visited the Peter-Paul fortress built by Peter the Great. It has a great wall, and prisoners once placed inside this wall were never known to have come out into the world again ... Then the Baroque church where all the Czars are buried—all of them, of course, but the last ... Within the vault only Peter the Great's tomb stands apart from the others, covered with flowers that are regularly laid on it.

Then from outside a vision of the svelte purity of the soaring bell tower rising above the ornate Baroque church.

From the Peter-Paul fortress to the Winter Palace on the 'fashionable' side of the Neva, and here also are the galleries known as the Hermitage.

Salon after salon of art treasures and magnificent chan-

152

deliers; and the Hermitage galleries with pictures from all the great European schools.

After lunching at my hotel I started on a ten-mile drive to see the first Summer Palace built by Peter and finished by Catherine. Small and perfect, it is situated in what was once an old village. Sloping, terraced Italian gardens; there is a waterfall from the little Palace's terrace way down to the Bay of Finland. The Germans looted and burnt every scrap of furniture, all the pictures, tapestries and treasures of three hundred years. The façade of the building, though, is unharmed, and they are busy resurrecting the inside. This Palace has a surround of beautiful woods—and it is interesting to record that some fine examples of architecture in the private grounds are the work of a Scotsman—Cameron by name.

The first six miles of the drive out from Leningrad was once a stretch of woods, felled though by the Moscow population for firewood during the cold winters of the war. There is one dramatic spot about three miles outside Leningrad—it was here that the Germans were finally halted. Now the whole countryside is gradually being built up again.

Tuesday 7th April

I enter the great Leningrad Choreographic School at ten a.m. It made me feel sad to drive up 'Theatre Street' (so gracefully described by Karsavina in her classic book) and to realise that in the great building I was about to enter there once lived all my European Russian Ballet friends ... I went to the children's first-year class under the direction of a pleasant young teacher. The children were very like our own; different, even physically, from the little Muscovites, who are more precocious and technically advanced at that age. I preferred this class; it was so much more fundamentally free from any artifice as there was no great emphasis on style or 'presentation' beyond their years. I found myself responding with an inner enthusiasm because its spirit was what I have always searched for and hoped to install in our own school.

153

I went on to Madam May's class; these fourteen-year-olds were just about the standard of our children in the same age group. Again, effort was on *work* before effect. There were two very talented children. Madam May proved to be an exceptionally strict teacher.

Midday found me watching the ballerina class under Zheleynova. A fine teacher; very elegant, and with a grand manner. Some beautifully trained dancers—gone was the Muscovite emotionalism—it was not unlike a ballerina class at the Royal Ballet. One exquisite young girl named Korgapkina showed perfect schooling firmly controlled. I felt inspired to find the principles that I still fight for at home so firmly established here.

In the afternoon I returned to the Hermitage and saw further schools of painting.

The evening was spent at the Kirov seeing *Laurencia* for the third time. Again, I prefer it to the Moscow version; simplified and a little more subtle, therefore the banalities that it contains are not so disturbing. Dudinskaya of the fabulous technique was dancing—although she is now forty-nine! I would have given much to have seen her fifteen years ago. There were two very fine young male dancers.*

Wednesday 8th April
Once more to the school at an early hour to see the boys' classes as well as the girls'. Boys' work very good. The girls' graduate class of this year was not as good as the Bolshoi class and I have already recorded that the Bolshoi class was by no means outstanding. I found these girls were too heavily built—and no doubt this was the basic trouble.

At one o'clock I had my promised interview with Lydia Lopokova's brother—Lopukhov. A dear old gentleman of seventy-three—now retired (except for a little choreography which we will not discuss).

* Rudolf Nureyev assures me that he was giving his first performance in the leading role that night. *N. de V.*

He is very like Lydia; the same nose, the same laugh and philosophical twist in his remarks.

He lives in a sort of 'grace and favour' flat in the school—there was an air about it of more favour than grace. It is situated off the hall; there is a tiny, scruffy little kitchen (no window) and then a small, very high room—but again no window. The four walls were lined with trays ... trays big and small, brass, tin and china, ancient and modern, round, square and oblong. It was a sight, this hobby of his—collecting 'trays' year in and year out! If I had only known in time I could have brought him one from England.

He is a reactionary—delights in quarrelling with everyone over policy, ballets and principles. But I liked him so much, with his fearless nonsensical attitude and his natural gaiety. One of the Bolshoi company asked my interpreter, 'How was Mr Lopukhov with Madam?' She assured him that the maestro was 'charming'. 'Thank goodness,' he said, 'she was lucky—he is generally so irritable with strangers.' I then realised that my earnest request to meet him had caused them some anxiety, but they were too polite to refuse me the interview.

After my visit I went to watch a rehearsal of *The Fisherman*. A remarkable work in the making by a young choreographer—Grigorovitch. The best choreography that I have seen so far; imaginative and poetic. We will hear more of him.

In the evening to the Hall of Culture to see a dance recital with choreography that was all by Jacobson, a man considerably older than Grigorovitch. The audience was rough and appeared to be rather devoid of 'culture', to use a word that is no longer used with any sense of discrimination. There was some good choreography, but the greater part of it was undistinguished. Many of the Kirov dancers appeared, and some of the younger ones are lovely artists.

Thursday 9th April
Classes again! A careful survey of the first and second-year children. I was deeply impressed and made several notes for

155

private consumption. On the whole the physical beauty of a Russian child shows a greater tendency to disappear in the older teenager than is to be observed in his or her English equivalent. Everyone in these two primary classes appears to be an embryo ballerina!

I follow up the classes by seeing *The Fisherman* in full. The run-through commenced at one p.m. following a very good class taken by Dudinskaya. (She is an excellent and original teacher. Her lesson is a true study in what I can only call 'choreographic pedagogy'—the art of class *enchaînements* that include the foundations of choreographic composition. This was also Legat's great gift.)

The third act of *The Fisherman* was spoilt by the usual propaganda touch that I imagine to be obligatory . . .

The fisherman is shown 'life' in a strange country run by capitalists; vice dens, street scenes, etc. He refuses to succumb, and, as far as I could make out—swam back to Russian shores!

(It is rumoured that the country is based on Japan—only this is a 'state' secret.)

Nevertheless, there still remained the young choreographer's remarkable invention. The 'Japanese' native movements were interesting and wonderfully interpreted—but politics won, and we had to submit to the inevitable down-grading to stress 'the message'.

I then spent some considerable time in the Theatre Ballet Museum. Very interesting; some records going back nearly two hundred years—I spotted a photograph of Cecchetti as a very young man.

It was a great relief to discover that there was no performance; I was very tired.

Friday 10th April
Back to school by ten a.m. Interview with the director at one p.m. He presented me with my eighth copy of Vaganova's book.

I had lunch in the school canteen, and then went to the little School Museum to meet the entire teaching staff at three p.m.

I was fortunate to have, as interpreter, an English girl studying in the school. They plied me with questions about our school, time-tables, hours of work—academic as well as balletic etc. They were very interested and gradually a series of discussions emerged. I think that the meeting was successful and that it led to a greater understanding of both schools and their relative problems.

I was also permitted to have a long conversation with the young choreographer, Belsky, an aesthetic-looking young man of thirty-two—looking about twenty-six. His great interest was in his English contemporary, Kenneth MacMillan! He is charming, very intelligent, and so eager to hear about other choreographers and their works. I told him everything I could in the time at my disposal about Balanchine, Massine and the Diaghilev Ballet—he was absorbed.

In the evening it was *Spartacus* with choreography by Jacobson. Very disappointed. I had liked his 'miniature' dances as they call recital numbers. But this was like an early de Mille 'epic' film on Rome in the days of slaves and gladiators.

I caught the midnight train back to Moscow; a superior edition of the first train. The sleepers were for two only; I shared mine with Madame Bocharnikova (director of the Bolshoi School), but my interpreter shared hers with a young man.

Saturday 11th April
We got back to the Embassy by nine thirty a.m. I stayed in all the morning unpacking and sorting out an endless list of names, in preparation for my letter writing to various directors etc.

Lunched with the Ambassador. At three o'clock I left for my 'conference' with the Bolshoi teaching staff. What did I find but a crowd of all grades of teachers, some prominent dancers and the six graduates of this year (eighteen to nineteen years of age). They were all eagerly awaiting a demonstration class on Royal Ballet School lines!

I felt that so much was at stake I just could not afford to

be nervous—in spite of the fact that I should have to teach without having had the opportunity to give the lesson any thought or preparation, and after a long all-night train journey ...

After a few minutes I felt a ripple of interest, and, with the help of my interpreter, and the fact that I could count up to ten in Russian and knew the Russian for 'left', 'right', 'again', 'good', 'you don't understand', I suddenly found it all quite easy. Of course the staff caught on to everything before the dancers (slightly dazed—but cooperative and intelligent), and echoed my instructions to them in their own language. Messerer produced a notebook and started writing the lesson down, all the arrangements of exercises, steps, etc. There was a real murmur of approval when I illustrated (in great detail) head, arms, etc., with every step, very often using the Cecchetti theory on this subject.

The girls responded fairly well, showing up, very naturally, certain of those weaknesses to be found in every school, however famous; but then the teachers had expressly asked me to do this as a matter of interest—we were not intending to concern ourselves with our approval or disapproval of any marked differences between us.

After it was all over, I realised that the lesson had aroused interest. I was particularly touched and honoured by Madame Kozhukhova. She is a contemporary of Madame Karsavina, yet she sat intently taking it all in. At the end she said to me, 'Such detail—it is something we have lost and we must put it back. I start at once ...'

A distinguished professor of anatomy was present and asked if he could talk to me. We were soon well away about the dancer's physique in general. I told him of my many superficial observations—slight anatomical defects possibly in the limbs, and how I noticed that they were in accord with certain physical points elsewhere in the body, facial bone structure, texture of hair, sloping or square shoulders etc. He kept smiling and nodding his head and at the end said, 'In my capacity as a professor I have observed much about dancers, but in your capacity as a teacher you seem to have observed some things that I am going to explore in theory—they are of extraordinary interest to me.'

Exhausted, I got back to the Embassy about six fifteen p.m. I dined with the Ambassador and a scientist just out from England. (It appears that we are about to have an extra attaché in the form of a scientist.) They went on to see an exhibition of American ice skating; earlier in the day I had asked to be excused—I was really very tired.

Sunday 12th April

My last day; I looked at my time-table. All letters to be written before eleven thirty; Bolshoi School performance of *Casse-Noisette* at the Little Theatre twelve o'clock to three; Lenin–Stalin tomb three fifteen. Dinner with Bolshoi leading teachers at Metropole Hotel five thirty ...

The *Casse-Noisette* was disappointing, except for the lovely 'Snow Flakes' choreography, which was also very well danced. Oddly enough the senior students showed more weakness in their style and interpretation than in their dancing. I suspect that general classroom discipline fades round about sixteen to seventeen. They are not ready, except in the case of a budding Ulanova, for so much freedom of expression; and certainly not at this moment, cut off as they are from outside contacts and comparisons with other countries' theatrical standards. The young dancer in the big *pas de deux* appeared to be singularly lacking in the most elementary production assistance.

After the performance my interpreter just said, 'The tomb! What will they say in England if you do not see it?' (She meant, of course, what would a Russian 'they' say to her if I did not.)

I realised that it was a matter of courtesy on my part to go with her as she was expected to report that she had taken me there—so off we went.

It was bitterly cold; there was a lot of snow on the ground but thank goodness the sun was shining. In spite of the privilege—as a foreign visitor—of joining a shorter queue, it took nearly three-quarters of an hour to get inside the mausoleum. You are spared little; the walk round the tomb is in the form of a square; two abreast, you cover three parts of the square at a distance of four feet from the bodies. They are encased in glass and the lighting is bright—embarrassingly bright. I think that for the Russians it is by now more of a curiosity visit than a true pilgrimage—more of a 'pilgrimage' perhaps for the members of the Republics—yet no doubt one way of spending a week in Moscow. On the way out my walk was so directed that I passed close under the Kremlin wall where ashes of revolutionary heroes are buried. There are three little tombs put up for two Englishmen and one American. These were carefully pointed out to me. 'How strange,' I said (I had had enough and was half frozen with cold). 'But surely you know them?' anxiously asked my interpreter. 'Of course not,' I said brightly. 'I have never heard of them—perhaps they left England a long time ago—I wouldn't know . . .' She was disappointed at the failure of such an exciting dramatic climax.

It aroused in me a sudden memory of Kruschev; my meeting with him on my first visit at a Kremlin cocktail party. It was explained to him that my mission was to look into an exchange of companies. 'Tell her,' he said, 'When England stops saying nasty things about Mr Kruschev our companies will make an exchange.' When they did, he sat in a box on the first night and exclaimed, 'Look at those girls—they might all be Russians.'

The dinner was presided over by a young woman representing the Ministry of Culture—she was a scientist. Only Madame Bocharnikova, Madame Gerdt and Mr Messerer were present. It was a delightful experience; I was again asked many questions; they were charming and asked me to forgive them, but they regarded me as the only part of the 'delegation' that belonged to them.

Speeches followed, of course, with allusions to breaking down

Two old prints of St Petersburg.
(Photographed by Donald Southern)

(Above): the opening night of the
Royal Ballet at the Kirov. (Photo:
Dominic)

(Below): the line-up at the last
night at the Bolshoi. (Photo:
Dominic)

Swan Lake—a performance given by
the Turkish State Ballet, with
Meriç Sumen as the Swan Queen.

(Above): *Çeşmebagi* (The Fountain):
choreography by Ninette de Valois.

(Below): the Turkish State Ballet
cast of *Coppélia* with the Shah of
Persia (centre) and the Turkish
Prime Minister, I. Inönü (right),
1962.

Diaghilev
'I have already placed on record
that I owe all my theatre
knowledge of the ballet to him.'

W. B. Yeats at the Abbey Theatre,
1932.
'I want you to come to Dublin and
help me revive my Plays for
Dancers ...'

The late Rudolf Benesh, whose notation is
installed in the state theatre ballet companies of
England, Scotland, Holland, Germany (Stuttgart
and Munich), Turkey, Canada, South Africa,
Australia, New Zealand, Norway and various
schools and institutions both in England and
overseas.

The boys of White Lodge.
(Photos: G. B. Wilson)

this and building up that. Messerer proposed my health and suddenly started to speak of my lesson—he said many nice things. But his approach was strictly technical and professional, and his manner never descended to any meaningless flattery. He said he had 'seen a teacher with personality, knowledge and a beautiful *ports de bras*,' and he added, with a twinkle, 'If Madam will excuse me—great intelligence.' Needless to say 'Madam' did excuse him. I felt positively light-headed. In my reply I was truthfully able to state that three weeks of inspiraton, adapting myself to a different approach, watching a great tradition at work, seeing what we had taken from it and what we should still take, realising happily that we also had some findings to offer—all these things had helped me to give a lesson that I now felt had not disappointed them.

On to the red, white and gold Bolshoi for the last time. It was *Don Quixote*, but bereft of all stars between the ages of twenty-six and thirty-six. This morning a hundred and twenty dancers had left by 'plane for New York. Tonight in Moscow this immense production was given without any visible effort!

It is a crude old ballet with a truly terrible score, and is served up with the same sort of performance. Lepeshinskaya was dancing like a magnificently animated virtuoso. She is their greatest technician. Wonderful feet, great surety, and in its own way a strong personality. I would love to have seen her ten years ago. She is still adored—it must be admitted that she can still dance, shunning no technical feat—the house shrieked its approval. She generally appears only at official party concerts. (Last time I was here her once influential husband was said to be undergoing temporary liquidation—I was told at the time that he was in prison. She still carried on though—tough—I saw her at that time in class, and no one would have imagined that she was in the midst of such trouble.)

I left for the airport after lunch accompanied by my interpreter, and the gentle and sincere Madame Bocharnikova as well as a 'Deputy Minister of Culture'. He presented me with a book on the Bolshoi Theatre.

161

All through this diary I have repeatedly alluded to 'my inter-preter', and so I would like to present a sketch of this woman of whom I became fond, and who went everywhere and did everything for me with the same degree of consideration and kindness that I received from everyone.

A strange little woman; she is a great prude submerged in communism along strict Party lines. I would call her a Crom-wellian character. Sexual love for her is almost taboo—an un-important pastime and unbinding 'because of its unreality to the material'. We spoke a great deal about books—her English readings are remarkable. They cannot buy any literature; she told me that she got everything she reads from the library. I told her I had a lot of books; I loved to collect them. 'Why?' she said. 'Haven't you got libraries?' 'Yes,' I replied, 'but one likes to own a favourite book.' 'Why?' she asked once more. 'You can go back to the library again ...'

On the day that we visited the University she remarked, 'You have seen all the palaces and houses of Princes; now you have seen what the Soviet Union can build—and once we used to be barbarians.' 'Oh,' I said, 'we have all been barbarians— do you know that 150 years ago in England you could be hanged for stealing a sheep?' 'And quite right too,' was her severe reply. 'You should be hanged for stealing a handker-chief ...' And then later—'We do not take life for murder— only for being a traitor to your country.' Still curious, I asked her why she felt so strongly about somebody stealing a handker-chief. 'Because it does not belong to you,' was the prompt reply.

Between the above remark and those on library books I detected a fanaticism—and a sincere one—concerning the needlessness and the danger of personal possessions; once an idealistic root that has now grown into a distorted tree.

Sometimes she was very touching; one day, during my end-less questions about treasures I saw in their churches, she looked at me—distressed and apologetic. 'Oh dear! I find it so hard to remember all your Christs!' Then she told me about her father's atheism, adding that her mother and grandmother

162

were strict Russian Orthodox and that her mother sometimes said, 'Oh, Ivan, do stop saying such things; if you go on so I will never be able to find you in the next world.'

As time wore on her iron curtain showed cracks in it, and the Party attitude was more relaxed. Seldom is a Russian unfriendly by nature; so she became, even under the dutiful execution of innumerable 'musts' and 'shoulds', suddenly human. She was intelligent and decided that she found me the same. She was oddly impressed with the class that I gave to the Bolshoi graduates ... 'You love your work, you are dedicated; you make everything so clear even to me as well as the others; and yet you could not speak to them in their language—so all could only be done by intense love and understanding.' Then on another day—'Everyone talks about your figure—but they do not see that your mind is controlling your figure.' I repeat these remarks to illustrate, alongside the preceding ones, the complexity of the mental process that was ceaselessly at work.

Her wartime experiences were harrowing to hear about. She was put on a train, bound for Siberia, with her mother and three younger sisters. The journey took four days; it was a bitter winter; little to drink and no food, excepting a tin of red caviare. Open trucks had to be used on the journey; hundreds of children with no parents travelled without any official papers. Many of these children were too young to know their names. 'We were not,' she said on reflection, 'very well organised.' They had no money on arrival in Siberia, even the children had to work.

Her descriptions of the Moscow winter when the Germans were closing in were terrible. Without food, except for a quarter of a loaf of bread a day; without fuel, except for what they could collect from the surrounding woods; without water, except for the ice that they fetched from the river and carried away in buckets—and all in thirty degrees of frost. The city was patrolled by men whose sole duty was to pick up those who dropped dead in the streets, generally on their way to the river for ice.

Her life as an official interpreter is devoted to using her knowledge of English in all directions and towards every form of art and science. She is indefatigable in her service, but you eventually feel that you are a mental patient who must never be left alone. When the official car called for me she was always with it; when I suggested (with nostalgic longing) that I could easily go back to the Pushkin Museum for an hour one morning before she called ... 'Alone? Never!' she gasped. 'Supposing something happened to you? It would be my fault, I am responsible.'

That is how it would be, of course; her fault. But the 'protection' among the hierarchy was, no doubt, not all devoted to kindly feelings. I was staying in a foreign Embassy, and they prefer their V.I.P.s in their own hotels.

I enjoyed to the full all the time that I spent with my fellow artists—a little world apart, inside a bigger world from which, of course, they receive many reminders of issues that are of more importance than their own. I often felt I was up against a force that was almost a 'religion' for a fanatical people and any form of argument was useless.

As the 'plane took off at the end of my visit I remember seeing rows of young fir trees stretching beyond the airport across the flat, white countryside. They appeared symbolic of the strange uniformity that had been imposed on everything. Yet this was the country that gave the world *War and Peace*, the book that surely stands alone in its greatness, the epic of a literary epic-producing century. Embracing everything; too far-reaching to fade; intensely human and full-blooded; yet its core holds the impregnable undying mysticism of the real Russian heart and mind.

But this soliloquy is apart from a great tradition in the theatre world—the Russian Ballet—to whom we in England owe such a debt, and further, so much gratitude to those Russian artists who have been in our midst for so long.

164

THE TURKISH STATE BALLET

... He'd invoke
The name of God mainly when his shoes hurt
But he was no sinner.

Sad road
For Suleyman Efendi
May God rest his feet!

'Epitaph for Suleyman Efendi'

(Extract from the Turkish poem by Orhan Veli Kanik, translated by
F. Stark)

We can claim, in the Turkish State Ballet, the first national ballet in Europe to have had its foundations laid by England.

I started the State Ballet of Ankara in a picturesque way in the autumn of 1947 on the shores of the sea of Marmara, close to the Istanbul airport. Here, in a primary school, the seed was sown; twenty-five seven-year-old children, boys and girls, were brought together and housed as the nucleus of the future ballet. At the end of the primary school years all the children had to be transferred to the Ankara State Conservatoire—and this practically amounted to a fresh start. Very few children followed the school to Ankara as the majority of the parents could not bear the idea of being separated from their children, and the distance between the two cities is about three hundred miles. To avoid the situation recurring, the Ankara State Conservatoire not only took into their middle school the half-dozen children who were prepared to leave Istanbul, it had also to set about holding auditions for a primary level intake in Ankara.

Both the Istanbul and the Ankara schools have been staffed by English teachers from the Royal Ballet and elsewhere. In 1948 Joy Newton and Audrey Knight went out to Turkey, in the first place to Istanbul for three years and then they moved to Ankara for one more year when the children were placed under the care of the Ankara Conservatoire. Next came Beatrice Appleyard, who is now married to the present director of the State Opera and Ballet, the distinguished pianist Mithat Fenmen. In 1955 Travis Kemp and Molly Lake went out as the principal teachers and directors of the Conservatoire School. They worked there for twenty years, and all the present dancers both in Turkey and abroad graduated under their tuition and guidance. For some years they were joined by Angela Bayley, who excels in the tuition of children.

The State Theatre Ballet also has a history of English names: those who have spent the longest period over there are Claude Newman (ex-Royal Ballet), Dudley Tomlinson (Royal Ballet and present teacher at Cape Town University School of Ballet), Richard Glasstone (Royal Ballet School). There have also been a host of 'guest' teachers, choreographers and *répétiteurs*. We now have resident Turkish conductors; but for eight years valuable pioneer work was done by Alan Abbot, the English conductor who is now with the Australian National Ballet.

The Ankara Conservatoire is a large, rambling building set around a wide courtyard, and here dozens of students of all ages studying drama, music and ballet are to be seen running, lounging and talking, or practising a musical instrument in a quiet corner. It can boast of its own theatre where an invited audience may see students from all branches of the Conservatoire giving performances. This Conservatoire is a remarkable achievement, in spite of the many shortcomings occasioned by 'laws' that need a new look. (In Turkey a law is not easily removed, yet broken it is known to be, in a way that is incomprehensible to the foreign mind.) The Conservatoire is run very much on the lines of our own state schools, and the academic course is nine years long. A 'diploma' is aimed at for graduation, but not always achieved. It has been found to be unrealistic to bar a dancer from the State Theatre for lack of the proper number of academic qualifications; quite a number leave once they have reached the age of eighteen, without distinguishing themselves academically. If their progress in the school is satisfactory, they join the company for one year as a student artist—they then have a further ballet test to pass, taken this time by the State Theatre staff.

We have, of course, to cope with certain inevitable difficulties. There is the eighteen months' military service and the very lucrative engagements that can be sought by the male dancers in Germany and even elsewhere. With the women it is different. Few, if any, wish to leave—they marry and settle down to a career in Turkey. It was, however, a difficult matter, during the first eight years, to convince the average family that the career of a dancer was possible to consider for women. When I first went out there it was, to many of the parents, an unthinkable pastime for a girl. The prejudice was exactly the opposite to that which was prevalent in England, for here we had to fight a prejudice over boys dancing. The Turks fought it over the girls. Therefore it is a matter for some satisfaction that the leading Turkish ballerina, Meric Sumen, returned to the Ankara State Ballet in the autumn of 1972 after giving performances of *Giselle* in Moscow, Leningrad and Kiev as a guest artist of the Soviet Union.

It will be of some interest to speak briefly about the Turkish State Ballet's domestic scene. In spite of the fact that their salaries are certainly low in comparison with other countries, they have a security offered to them that is unknown as yet to their English and American contemporaries. Everything is

167

found for them during their nine years at the Conservatoire, and on graduation any dancer, singer, or actor of an average talent, can look forward with some surety to a permanent job for life and a pension on retirement. If they go abroad for good the money that they have to refund towards the expenses of their nine years of studies is very modest. It can be paid off out of a lucrative engagement of one year's standing elsewhere.

Of course every positive has its negative. If, as a dancer, you are lazy and have no real incentive to work, there is no 'law' recognising dismissal for (a) non-attendance, or (b) refusal to dance certain roles. It is left to the staff to report such happenings and fines seem to be the only answer, but a reduction in the monthly salary is no solution—therefore in the end everyone hesitates to report. With a certain irony I can recall two young Turkish dancers at a Martha Graham rehearsal: 'No one has *talked*,' whispered one dancer. 'They dare not,' was her companion's reply, 'they have not got permanent contracts.' But general discipline over the years has made very marked progress.

I can speak with enthusiasm about Turkish dancers; about the talent of those who really *are* talented. Many of the principals and soloists stand up well to their contemporaries elsewhere. The general standard of the *corps de ballet* in comparison is not yet so high; the reasons for the moment are obvious. It has been a rushed job to turn out the necessary numbers, and therefore the choice of intake over the years has not always been as selective as it will be in the future.

Turkish dancers have, in the last sixteen years, managed to dance their way through a formidable number of English works: they include *Les Patineurs, Les Rendezvous, Pineapple Poll, Beauty and the Beast, Checkmate, The Rake's Progress, Solitaire, Les Sylphides, The Burrow* and *Blood Wedding*. They have also given the following classics: *Coppélia, Le Lac des Cygnes, The Sleeping Beauty* and *Giselle*. Other full-length ballets are *Romeo and Juliet* (choreographer Alfred Rodriques) and *Prince of the Pagodas* (choreographer Richard Glasstone); and in the autumn of 1973 a spirited account of Ashton's *La Fille Mal Gardée* certainly stretched every resource to its limits. One brief conversation may paint the necessary picture:

Question: Have you ever flown anyone on this stage?

Answer: Yes—once.

Question: How was it?

Answer: She had to go to hospital.

It was then decided to 'fly' the umbrella—instead of the artist concerned. Otherwise all was well, with good dancing and orchestral playing, and admirably executed scenery and costumes. It is also interesting to record that a performance of this ballet was given by a visiting Italian ballet company in Istanbul one hundred and fifteen years ago.

In the summer of 1973 Turkey's National Ballet broke new ground: it staged a full evening of four Turkish one-act ballets with Turkish music—two of them choreographed by two young Turkish choreographers, Oytun Trufando and Duygu Aykal.

But there is another development that seems to move forward without any interest shown on the part of foreigners whose duties should include the recording of such matters. When I went out there in 1947 Turkey was not on the 'touring list' of any European or American ballet company. This is hardly the case today, for the growing interest over the years has changed the picture. Companies from other countries now tour Turkey every year. Apart from obvious appearances in the Ankara and Istanbul State Theatres there are some wonderful open air theatres—Istanbul, Izmir and Ephesus—to quote three of the famous ones of the moment. With a seating capacity of seven to ten thousand such 'dates' are rewarding for visiting companies. Apart from the English, Turkey has welcomed American, French, Belgian and Russian companies; slowly they are finding their way to this new land of the ballet, and I think that the efforts of the Royal Ballet and others should be remembered by companies from both Europe and America that can now add Turkey to their European tours.

The Turks are to be congratulated for their courage and their determination to make the ballet a part of their state theatre policy. They may require in the arts, for some time yet, the *impetus* of foreign aid—rather more than its actual practical help. It is the temperament of the people; it cannot be changed overnight, only influenced over the years. One must remember that their present lack of self-reliance has nothing to do with any lack of intelligence, talent or ability to fulfil any task set them; they have yet to prove to their own satisfaction in the theatre that they can lead themselves, and cease to turn to the foreigner again and again through a natural mistrust of their abilities in relation to themselves.

Moreover, they are, as yet, some way behind the rest of Europe in one important respect: the older generation do not always show sufficient faith in youth. The young are given every possible opportunity to *study*; scholarships, state grants and bursaries are pretty lavish, but when the elders are afterwards confronted with a request for some form of self-expression, youth may find the barricades of age all along the way. There is here the shadow of the country's veneration for age and the wisdom that is always presumed to accompany it, and this attitude can sometimes prove to be as impregnable as the law.

Slowly over the years there has emerged a Turkish staff of teachers and *répétiteurs*, ballet mistresses, ballet masters and notators—and now it is to be the turn of the choreographers. I have been anxious to see them absorb not only the traditional classical ballets, but also a series of modern works; and thus, now that they have begun to create their own ballets, they have a professional yardstick with which to measure their efforts.

When one reflects on the rich and varied quality of their National dances, it takes the imagination one step nearer the future. A vision appears of the evolution of their choreography in the hands of those artists who will have the technical prowess to bend their traditional heritage to serve their theatre—and with a result that will have its roots in the Turkish scene.

Some twelve years ago the Shah of Persia visited Turkey and attended a gala performance given by the Turkish Ballet in his honour. There was, subsequently, a request for me to start up a similar effort in Teheran.

I made several visits; it was slow work as the theatre scene in general was nothing like as advanced as it was in Turkey, and for some years the building of the Opera House was temporarily suspended.

Today the Persian Folk and National Dance Teams are under the direction of Robert de Warren, and there is a ballet attached to the opera.

* * *

I can recall that as a child of about ten years of age I was asked to dance in a London drawing-room for the entertainment of a visiting Persian Prince. He gave me a dancer's charm, an exquisite tiny gold coin that had engraved on one side (in Persian) the words 'Allah guide thy feet'.

They were guided to the shores of Asia Minor in no uncertain fashion some thirty-five years later.

DIAGHILEV

It is not revolutions and upheavals
That clear the road to new and better days
But revelations, lavishness and torments
Of someone's soul, inspired and ablaze.

Pasternak: 'After the Storm'

So many people today have discovered how well they knew Diaghilev. Who really 'knew him'? Possibly nobody.

So how will I write about this man when I have no more real authority to do so than half of the people who have already written about him? I must confess that it is my third effort, and this time I shall attempt no more than sharply recollected incidents, sketchily sketched observances. I have already placed on record that I owe all my theatre knowledge of the ballet to him.

I will first mention his remarkable head. Well-shaped but enormous. Sometimes when he was crossing our rehearsal rooms I had a fleeting impression that he was tottering, but the effect was due to this particular piece of outsize bone structure, the only part of him that was too big for his boots. Then came the eyeglass, distinguished, flattering, and no doubt useless.

But everything could be blotted out by the voice. The voice was not, as is said, 'worthy of the man'. It was too high-pitched to match his frame, and as a young member of the company

172

I was used to hearing it grumble in a querulous fashion, or pitched several tones higher in an outburst of rage. It always struck me that he moved as someone in a hurry, yet he sat in a chair as someone who never meant to get up again; he appeared to be static, but the general effect achieved was one of a dignified air of permanency.

He noted things on his own, sometimes very small things; he noted rather more things pointed out by his alternatively devoted and exasperated entourage.

One morning he suddenly appeared flanked by Poulenc and Kochno at a very embryo *Les Biches corps de ballet* rehearsal. I was quick to note the reason, for Poulenc was convinced, and had told me so, that I was the best little 'Biche' of all the little 'Biches'. I felt myself being singled out, no doubt as the New English Girl. The efforts of my two fans seemed to be falling— as far as I could note out of the corner of an anxious eye—on deaf ears, a misty eyeglass, and a deadly bored face ... but suddenly we had arrived at my favourite sequence. The great head nodded, the big mouth grinned, and he tottered out (or so it seemed) followed by the triumphant entourage. Sequel: Nijinska choreographed her role of the Hostess on me.

At a party in London during a Coliseum season the ladies of the company attended in full evening dress; I wore a white dress of *The Great Gatsby* epoch with an artificial flower pinned on it—a fashion of that time. Suddenly I saw the awe-inspiring finger beckoning me. I obeyed the summons expecting the worst. On arrival there was a pause as an index finger delicately touched the flower, and the head seemed to wander all over my dress. There was then what I recall as a discreet, fastidious whisper, 'You have good taste, my dear.' The remark was a dismissal, not a reception, for the head had left me before the end of the sentence to direct the eyeglass to loftier things.

My glass of champagne afterwards tasted like a dull sedative following a moment of superb elation ...

I was not always so successful. He hated to give his auto-graph. At another supper party in the famous room at the top of Her Majesty's Theatre I dared to present him with my menu to sign. A pause—this time a distasteful one—and then he wrote 'No, no, Nanette' and made an indecipherable 'D' underneath it. (The musical of that name was running at the Palace.)

His entourage always intrigued me, for one had a feeling that for half of the time they were acting as a reprimanding body-guard. When I first joined the company Benois and others of the Imperial Ballet era were prominent in our midst. Benois was in fact executing costumes and décor for certain operas that Diaghilev was directing for the Monte Carlo Opera season. Some of these older artists certainly asserted themselves, as they felt (and quite rightly) that they had 'launched' him when in St Petersburg in his younger days. It was all rather like a lot of established ballerinas of a slightly senior age bowing out in submission at the arrival of a young Fonteyn. A moment would come when, in unison, they would say, 'she really must not do it that way again.'

But the most interesting administrative full-time member of the staff was the young Boris Kochno. We were good friends and I learnt a great deal by talking to him and watching him at work, for he had perfect taste and a wonderful sense of pro-portion. His devotion to the mind and matters of the Master was untiring, and Diaghilev leant on his judgement more and more. I think this was because, progressive as Diaghilev was, he was a great traditionalist at heart, and Kochno had been taught to think likewise. (In my opinion his direction of *La Syl-phide* for the Roland Petit Company soon after the war culmi-nated in the best production we have seen, not even excepting the Danish version.) It has been said that through worry, ill-health, and the loss of the full-blooded glory of the past, Diaghi-lev was becoming more interested in smaller experimental works. It was rumoured that he contemplated handing over the big company to Kochno and continuing himself, on experi-mental lines, with a small one. No doubt this report gave birth to the stories about his 'search for lost youth'. If the idea had materialised it is my belief that the Diaghilev Ballet would have continued unchallenged up to the Second World War and after. Kochno was his heir, not Colonel de Basil.

Diaghilev liked the English but never really took the trouble to understand them, no doubt it was not the sort of trouble that he found worthwhile. One day after an argument with one of them he was heard to murmur, 'Sometimes it seems that God only made animals and the English.' But he did admire English dancers and believed in their future.

His wit was generally satirical and consequently tinged more than often with a touch of malice. It was exasperation that turned it on just as tranquillity turned it off. Once, discussing one dancer with another, he summed up: 'Well, the difference between the two of you is that if she were accused of a murder she had *not* done, everybody would want to prove she had done it; but if you were accused of a murder you *had* done—everyone would try and prove you hadn't.'

Humour was not often to be noted, by me anyway; Lord Berners played a practical joke on him that was not only a colossal failure, it scared and offended Diaghilev. Yet he used to love to watch Balanchine miming the old 'Grandfather of the Fair' on the balcony in the first scene of *Petrushka*. It was a part you had to make up as you went along, and Balanchine used to make tremendous jokes with the beard which delighted Diaghilev.

He could be kind and sympathetic, and on the whole was just in his dealings with the company. He awaited them all graciously at the top of a mental flight of stairs, with a patient understanding as to the fact that most of them would remain at the bottom out of his reach. He had favourite artists, both male and female, and here he never failed to sense things correctly about all of them—with a judgement far ahead of his staff. If circumstances caused him to engage anyone that he did not like, God help such an intruder, for no one else could do so. 'Why, oh why,' he would wail over two sets of married couples, 'did they have to marry that way round?' He had only wanted one of the men and one of the women and not their respective spouses.

175

He was often accused of dilettantism. It was partly true and he was known to have admitted to it. People were engaged for one job, and, often through the friendly offices of the 'entourage', gave further service when possible in the *corps de ballet*. They cropped up in static peasant roles and as 'mothers'. The climax was reached when his very intelligent secretary got herself involved in the back row of *Les Sylphides*. Some of us were vocally indignant. A great number of the *corps de ballet* were, and always had been, unbelievably bad dancers. All the soloists worked in the big ensembles, they had to, but their presence was no yardstick by which to judge the non-soloists.

Diaghilev's love of the traditional was shown sometimes in quite trivial ways. Some time after I had left the company he asked me to come and see him. He had an engagement at La Scala, Milan, and wanted me to come to Italy for one week, just to dance the 'finger variation' in *The Sleeping Beauty* and the Pizzicato in the *pas de trois*. I had to decline, but I found his enthusiasm over this argument very touching. 'Think,' he said, 'you will be able to say that you have danced at La Scala.' I remember thinking that if I could not add 'with the Russian Ballet' it would not be regarded as so glamorous!

A vision of the autocrat sailing to that point of no return: his row with Nijinska over an additional scene, a front cloth one, that he wanted inserted in her one-act ballet of *Romeo and Juliet*. Constant Lambert, who had written the music, sided with the choreographer. According to Constant, Diaghilev threw a scene closely resembling an epileptic fit, he was so angry. He had his way, Balanchine was ordered to choreograph the extra scene. As Sokolova was taken ill I was put on to play the nurse, and I can remember performing the new scene that had been choreographed without any music.

I am now about to stray into a land of supposition, inspired by a query that rose in my mind when Sergueeff, in 1932, said to me bitterly, 'Diaghilev's Ballet! It was ours.'

Of course, Diaghilev had the advantage of the resources that had emerged from the Imperial Ballet. He was even able to take the company wholesale to Europe for summer seasons before the Revolution. He was able to collect the same artists as lost, wandering souls after the *débâcle*. For years, then, he had behind him a great root from which could spring his ideas and their development. Interesting to imagine what would have happened if at the start he had been faced with a vacuum; interesting also to imagine the possible plight of ballet if he had not been there to influence a considerable portion of this root when it was in danger of becoming driftwood through no fault of its own.

It is fascinating to wonder still further. We cannot visualise what the consequences would have been if there had been no revolution that resulted in Russia overthrowing everything. Fascinating to wonder if the artistically revolutionary ideas, already very much astir among the Imperial Ballet artists as well as others (including Diaghilev) during the first years of the twentieth century, would have continued to be developed progressively, if Imperialism had given the necessary lead to both its country and its theatre.

It was Diaghilev's Russian entourage that undoubtedly guided his footsteps during the first years in Russia; that he outstripped them and replaced them later with such artists as Picasso, Braque and the avante-garde of Paris goes without saying, but did his second period (1919 to 1929) give us any real development of Russian Ballet? Economically speaking the question is an unfair one, for it was not possible to attempt things on the same scale, and geographically we must not forget that they were an émigré company with no headquarters, save a sojourn of four months in Monte Carlo every winter.

The result is, in point of fact, that only a few of the ballets of the second period have lived, and they are all of an international flavour with the exception of *Les Noces* and the charming *Contes Russes*, and the latter did not survive the era. We must remember that the 'root' helped him once more with the discovery of Balanchine at the Empire Theatre in 1925.

*   *   *

'Death of the Russian Ballet' wrote Ernest Newman as the heading to his article on *The Sleeping Beauty* in 1921. Diaghilev was 'touché' for he was aware of Newman's outspoken support of the Massine repertoire and the Stravinsky ballets. He (Diaghilev) wrote somewhat fulsomely about Tchaikovsky, and was sharply reprimanded by more than one musical critic. But the London public rallied to him when *Les Noces* was attacked. (One evening paper's musical critic remarked, 'If this is a Russian wedding, God preserve us from a Russian funeral.') Printed pamphlets of protest at the press reception, signed by H. G. Wells, descended on the audience from the gallery. Great days!

Diaghilev was said to revel in theatre demonstrations. A favourite of his was the one that we had to live through in Paris on the first night of Nijinska's one-act ballet *Romeo and Juliet*. Almost immediately after the opening the curtain had to come down for peace to be restored. We then started the ballet again. Meanwhile Diaghilev walked up and down in the wings smiling to himself . . .

Was this the dilettante? The gnomic impresario? The man searching for lost youth? The man at the summit gazing down on the earthbound?

It was none of these things. It was just Diaghilev.

WILLIAM BUTLER YEATS

It is significant that when physical violence is to be
represented in these plays, Yeats represented it in a
stylised manner with dance-steps and drumbeats.
Every device—and lack of device—is employed to
keep the play inside a crystal.

Extract from The Poetry of W. B. Yeats *by Louis MacNeice*

Sligo, August 1969. A small Irish town with its familiar late
Georgian houses. Familiar also the busy rushing river, for such
waters are never far from an Irish town, and generally manage
to tumble through it, as is the case in Sligo.

What was Sligo doing in the summer of 1969, so painfully
near to the turmoil that had already started on the other side
of the border? It was holding one of its Yeats International
Summer Schools run by the Yeats Society of Sligo, and I had
had the honour of being asked to address those members of the
Society who were attending the summer school of this particular year.

When I entered the packed hall to give my address I felt that
I was back in America on a lecture tour, for here in Sligo I
found myself facing a crowd of people of which at least two-
thirds were Americans. I was reminded of the fact that whenever I had found my lectures on the ballet hanging fire in the
States, I had always switched to W. B. Yeats and his Plays for

Dancers, and when I further announced that I had known him and worked for him, there was a great reawakening on the part of my audience, sometimes accompanied by audible gasps of wonderment. This pilgrimage to Sligo on the part of the poet's ardent American followers was no surprise to me, I was anyway used to a regular flow of letters from American university students saying that they were writing a thesis on the Irish poet, W. B. Yeats, and would I help them by answering some questions . . . in the last few years I have noticed a tendency for the same request from English students.

The last year or two has brought forth a great deal of writing and broadcasting about the poet, and some efforts made to stage his Plays for Dancers. Much emphasis and discussion has been devoted to his 'symbolism' and 'mysticism'. Dare I say perhaps, interesting and significant as this aspect of the poet is known to be, the whole matter is being somewhat over-played? We are in danger, I feel, of not being able to see the wood for the trees. A great poet sings to us from his heart, and how his heart arrives at all the wonderment that it finds is a matter of vision; it has more strength left alone, left wrapped in its own mystery, and he would mean us to absorb the ulti-mate with the accent on a sublime and contented acceptance of any one of his sequence of words. That he wrote of his ex-perience did not mean the necessity of a prolonged and painful analysis of how he may or may not have applied them to his poetry.

'All the excitements in my life go on in my head,' he once said to me. But mercifully they escaped and reached the fool-scap page to receive the world's acclaim.

Yeats had always felt the call of movement in relation to his writings, and he felt the same draw towards music. But he did not show any active interest in music and dance as arts in their own right. For him it was the call of the rhythm of the body, and musicality of words, the search for a fusion in a unified expression of his dance dramas, symbolic in the oneness of the mystery that surrounded his great vision. In design he was often

180

wonderfully served by Edmund Dulac. Dulac's designs were austere and very pure, with a penetrating intellectual approach, and such designs seemed to me much more in sympathy with Yeats' intentions than Gordon Craig's were. The influence on Yeats' dance in the theatre came from the Noh plays of Japan; it would, I think, be fairer to say that here he found an example at work of his deeply-sensed theatrical conception, enhanced by the Japanese dancer, Ito, who performed for him in his first experiments.

Yeats' early experiments were in the drawing-rooms of London and Dublin houses, and later when the urge returned to make the effort again, the little Peacock Theatre was built alongside the Abbey Theatre of the late 1920s. By then Ito had returned to Japan and the Abbey was very much 'the Establishment' of the Irish drama scene, with its repertoire of successful Irish peasant plays written by distinguished Irish dramatists of the day, the only subsidised state theatre in Great Britain and the only state company to visit America for long tours.

We all know the part that human contacts play in our individual development, and my encounter and subsequent work with W. B. Yeats rates high in my personal list of inspiring influences. He was on a visit to the Festival Theatre, Cambridge, in 1926, where he had come to see a play by the poet Gordon Bottomley. I had helped in the staging of it, and had also shown some miniature choreographic works of my own. He asked to meet me as he had been very moved by what he had seen of my work on this occasion. We met the next morning in the dim foyer of the theatre. Always I can recall the great dark figure sitting in profile. Yeats had a curious habit of not looking at his companion during a conversation. He would look down or up or remain, as in this case, in profile. The voice was warm, rich with a mighty resonance of its own. He always conversed with conviction and inspiration, and you remained quite unperturbed that you were not included in his line of vision. There was a cartoon, once famous in Dublin, of Yeats and his great friend, A. E. Russell, setting out in Merrion Square to visit each other. They were portrayed as ships that pass in the night, for one always contemplated the sky above him and the other the earth beneath.

I could see before the conversation started that he had come to a decision and that it was for me to listen and accept, and then to be led. The opening was both simple and direct: 'I want you to come to Dublin to help me revive my Plays for Dancers which must now be restaged and put back into the Dublin scene.'

I was only working at that time for repertory theatres as it was the period of my long wait, after leaving the Diaghilev Ballet, for the further development of the Old Vic. The idea filled me with both joy and excitement, for I had a veneration for Ireland's National Theatre. He went on to tell me that he was not satisfied, he thought that the Abbey was in a groove, he wanted to see poetic drama encouraged, to establish something that was far removed from the conventional plays that they were endlessly performing. There was a further matter behind this movement that was not only a very good incentive but one that roused Yeats' fighting spirit. The Gate Theatre was about to open in Dublin under two energetic producers of the younger school. This was felt to be a challenge to the Abbey, and, although the latter was the undisputed National Theatre, it was Yeats—out of all the Abbey governors—who wanted to take up the challenge of this vital movement that was about to be accepted in the city of Dublin. He would always react in this way, for he had a love of what I can only call the moving thought, the progress and the 'excitement' of the mind. Yet a certain philosophical caution prevailed that was illustrated in the following remark made to me: 'They can afford to be wholly experimental, for they have no traditions.'

Lennox Robinson—the Irish playwright and the devoted right hand of Yeats in the general running of the Abbey—was the one who had to cope with this new idea. He was a character of charm, humour and integrity. ('I love a row as long as I am not in it', was his prompt reply once to a hint that a row was brewing.) Lennox's account to me of what followed the poet's visit to the Festival Theatre was highly entertaining. One morning his front door bell was impatiently rung. It was pouring with rain, and standing outside in the downpour was Yeats who never moved until he had imparted all the news about his proposed new venture to his bewildered co-director.

The sequel was swift. A teacher (the actress Vivienne Bennett) went to Dublin to direct a group of dancers and I paid two or three visits a year to help mount and perform Yeats' Plays for Dancers and to give performances of miniature ballets.

I found that the whole approach to these special play productions at the Abbey Theatre was something that I had never experienced in England, and on my part a great deal of adaptation was necessary both as a dancer and as a choreographer.

The native attitude to the realisation of these plays was one of extreme simplicity. At certain moments the scene would become completely static. I had already noted the wonderful coordination between the players in the theatre's straight plays. In these Plays for Dancers the production merely highlighted this strange sense of interplay, and this is also evident in the Noh plays of Japan, although their technical approach with its ageless tradition is more involved. This gift of Celtic understatement proved to be masterly when a work included music, words, song and dance.

Time and time again I have been asked to analyse and give a picture of what these productions were like. It is almost an impossible task. I can state, though, that you had to feel more than understand; you had to allow yourself to be absorbed into the whole, never to exist as an isolated part, only as a part of the whole. It became more and more a question of feeling the play rather than intellectually trying to understand every line. In the end there was a fusion; you felt your body and your emotions take part in the spirit of the general production. There was its intense simplicity, its purity, the direct appeal to feeling, and its poetry. I gave up trying to understand many moments, instead I accepted and became absorbed. In certain passages I was reminded of the poet's own words:

> I have bid you turn
> From the cavern of the mind

That was exactly what one did, for it was the only way of arriving. In these plays one developed a very strange and moving reaction to the poet, the strength of the stilled mind, devoid of anything but the purity of a deep inner meaning that was not capable of expression in the concrete terms of everyday speech. It was not the theatre that I knew, there was none of the theatrical effects, theatrical approaches that I was used to. Symbolism was there, but as a symbol. There was no tortuous breakdown ordering you to return to the cavern of the mind and turn it into a research laboratory. Again to find a parallel we recall the Noh players.

We played in masks, both actors and dancers. Here was a nobility of form that added to the remote objective feeling of the whole venture, for the mask was the outward and important symbol of this inner force that was at work. My mask never worried me, for its presence became all-important. They were beautiful masks and caught the spirit of the poet's dream world. I always studied my masks very carefully, and then I knew what I had to express with my movements so as to illustrate both action and meaning. In the end I just felt that my face was a part of the mask's own projection.

The effect of these productions on the public was very interesting. The majority who attended were a specialised public who had known about these plays for many years, yet we knew that others were slowly seeking out the theatre to sample these things. We had many nights when the vision of Yeats, intangible as it was, became a unifying effort between players and audience, when the quiet and the calm that we had accepted during the production now swept also through the audience and we were completely one; nights when the playing of the players and the watching of the playgoers was made

184

aware of the far-reaching exploration of a poet's mind. This liaison produced an unearthly quietness, but never a sense of deadness.

Among the younger school of our immediate past, Beckett, I would say, achieved the first approach in the same direction, but strictly through the eyes of his own generation. I refer to his *Waiting for Godot*. The production in London was too self-conscious, too fussy, too much effort went into it. A little later I saw the play in Ireland, in a tiny theatre in Dun Laoghaire. This was enlightening, for it was effortless and timeless. Would London have thought, in this presentation, that Dublin had not bothered? Possibly. But the whole play stressed the acceptance of things that are meant or not meant to happen, nor did it permit undue emphasis on truth as we generally see it—just one half of a whole.

I have never understood the general lack of comment on Yeats' enigmatic humour. He had a subtle sense of irony enhanced by his trick of intoning his remarks. 'It will be called "Portrait of the Poet in his Last Long Illness",' he would murmur, gazing at Augustus John's famous painting of him sitting in a chair covered with rugs. People, simple people, could interest him intensely, and he would tell about an acquaintance of no particular renown in a way that would highlight the shrewdness and the humane quality of his reaction to his fellow men. Intolerance was reserved for those of greater powers. Of H. G. Wells he once said to me fiercely, irrevocably, 'That man has the mind of a machine.' Finish! I never dared mention him again ...

The poet had a curious practical streak in him, and this is not uncommon in a highly creative man. He always sought for progress; he sensed that the theatre could not afford to stand still, and he would make terse, wise and sometimes very humorous remarks. When a pessimist said to him, 'You may build your Irish theatre, produce your Irish players, but how are you going to keep them in the country?' 'I won't have to try,' was the prompt reply, 'the Dublin accent will do it for me.'

One day I was in the office when Yeats came in from a Senate meeting. The general air in Dublin was of bitter indignation, for there had been an outburst of the all too fashionable telephone tapping, and a private conversation between Yeats and a friend on the matter of censorship had reached the press. Only Yeats remained calm and philosophical, and although one suspected a secret enjoyment of the general fuss, he dismissed it all with, 'At one time it was done for patriotic reasons and today it is just a bad habit.'

Two memories stand out that are as clear as my first picture of Yeats in 1926 . . .

A vivid early summer afternoon in Lennox Robinson's garden on the shores of Dalkey Bay. Yeats is there, and Sheila Richards, one of The Abbey's leading actresses. The poet recites his poems from memory amidst the summer sounds. When Lennox wrote to me after Yeats' death he recalled that magic hour with the words, 'For we have seen Shelley plain.'

My last memory of him is a sad one. We met in Liverpool about 1934 when I had to tell him that I could no longer come to Ireland because of my increasing responsibilities at Sadler's Wells. 'And who,' he said, gazing elsewhere as usual, 'will do my Plays for Dancers?'

Undeserved—in the light of all the experience that working in Plays for Dancers gave me—was the gentle tribute to me in his dedication of 'Queen of the Great Clock Tower'.

> To Ninette de Valois
> asking pardon for covering
> her expressive face with a mask

It was no mask in the conventional sense of the word that covered my face. I was certainly behind a mask, but able to dance in complete unison with what was covering my face, and both the mask and the dance sprang from the vision of one of the world's greatest poets.

186

WHAT MAKES A DANCER'S LIFE

Dancing Rightly

And all these proportionate strengths and measured efforts of the bough produce its loveliness, and ought to be felt, in looking at it, not by any mathematical evidence, but by the same fine instinct which enables us to perceive, when a girl dances rightly, that she moves easily, and with delight to herself; that her limbs are strong enough, and her body tender enough, to move precisely as she wills them to move. You cannot say of any bend of arm or foot what precise relations of their curves to the whole figure manifest, in their changeful melodies, that ease of motion; yet you feel that they do so, and you feel it by a true instinct. And if you reason on the matter further, you may know, though you cannot see, that an absolute mathematical necessity proportions every bend of the body to the rate and direction of its motion, and that the momentary fancy and fire of the will measure themselves, even in their gaily-fancied freedom, by stern laws of nervous life, and material attraction, which regulate eternally every pulse of the strength of man, and every sweep of the stars of heaven.

From Ruskin Today—An Anthology *by Kenneth Clark*

(The following article appeared in the *Sunday Telegraph*: November–December, 1963.)

I

There still exists the idea that the ballet is a precarious profession for boys. Nothing could be further from the truth. As the situation stands today it is a far more rewarding profession for the boys than it is for the girls. For one thing, it is the male dancers that we are asked for by national institutions all over Europe to fill appointments as teachers, directors and choreographers. These countries have the old tradition that the ballet is led by the male artist.

Women are splendid pioneer workers. Pioneering gives full play to their sense of dedication, detail, intuition and fanaticism. The picture, though, is bound to change. Dedication has to develop objectivity of outlook, detail submitted to a fair balance between the part and the whole, intuition turn to logical reasonings and fanaticism give way to the acceptance of reality.

It is essential that we realise that the real history of ballet— and by this I mean its creative work, its organisation, its pedagogy—has been a history of great male choreographers, directors and teachers.

Diaghilev always said that no woman could be as great a choreographer as a man because it was impossible for a woman to be as masculine in a movement required of a man, as it was for a man to be feminine in a movement required of a woman.

Above all, in England we want these historical facts understood and accepted. We want the public to realise that once again the development of ballet is rapidly passing into the care of the mature male element.

My experience with the Diaghilev Company in the 1920s had shown me that here was a group of people brought up in a great tradition in their own country. They were certainly refugees when I knew them, and in circumstances that they did not regard as particularly secure. Yet their conditions struck me as being exceptionally good. At least everyone worked for ten

188

months in the year. We had nothing to touch such security in England.

I wanted a tradition and I set out to establish one. I did not contemplate it to be anything very experimental, new or exciting. I just wanted to establish this. I even imagined that our dancers would branch off in experimental work of their own— and there are signs now of this happening.

Instinct told me (or was it a very feminine preoccupation with security?) that some sort of livelihood must be fought for and obtained before anything could really be done for our aspiring dancers. Where was I to look for the necessary bricks and mortar to establish a tradition and offer to the artists the foundation of their economic security? Certainly not to the commercial theatre, because of the expense and because its leaders did not visualise any popular support for ballet.

I stormed the Old Vic armed with an introduction to 'The Lady' Lilian Baylis, manager of Sadler's Wells. I was convinced that within her theatre lay our only hope. It was for another four years I had to watch the slow building of the Sadler's Wells Theatre, before a young English ballet company had a roof over its head.

I had to hand over to the theatre my private school and its annual income in return for a rehearsal room and contracts to six girls at £2 10s a week to dance in the opera ballets. That was the simple and unspectacular birth of what is now the Royal Ballet.

Bricks and mortar were the foundation of economic security for our dancers: fulfilment, however, lay in the long-term career structure afforded to them.

What jobs are there that will extend the careers of these retiring dancers? Some dancers obviously show the pedagogue's mind, and they will make good teachers. Quite early in their careers, even when they are still at school, we can spot those who have an aptitude for exam work, who understand the theory of dancing very well, and who have the ability and the authority to impart their knowledge.

189

Then again there is the boy or girl who shows a flair for *répétiteur* work—that is, the ability to coach and rehearse people. They are the ones who if asked in school to show a step or a movement will do so with a clarity and simplicity that everybody can understand and follow. From quite an early age one can therefore mark down future ballet masters, *répétiteurs* and teachers. And to this list must be added the notation writers—those highly skilled in the art of writing down ballets in 'shorthand'. The rarest to find, of course, is the choreographer, who possesses the gift of creating, of turning the steps of the dance into the poetry of movement. Such a one is born and not made.

Not that there is anything automatic or mechanical about being a good dancer. I shall show how good physique and technical ability, vital as they both are to the dancer, are in themselves insufficient without natural talent.

I do have a rather practical mind and I hate disorder and lack of method. Born and brought up in Ireland, I have always noticed how the Irish have tidy minds but untidy characters. By throwing myself into organisation I have perhaps succeeded in exorcising some of those Irish traits.

Perhaps it is just as well that teaching, choreography and organising are my passionate interests in ballet. Knowing what I do now of the physique and talent demanded of the very best dancers, I may perhaps be grateful that for me dancing for the sake of dancing was never the consuming interest.

II

The dance is founded on the natural laws of movement. Few people realise that there is little that is not, in its essence, a perfected movement of everyday life, and is based on the anatomical structure of the body. I have always believed that the old ballet masters, responsible for the elementary exercises we carry out today, must have had an astonishing knowledge of anatomy.

Ballet is first of all concerned with the conception of what can be attained through the development of a perfect body—

or one as near perfection as nature permits. If a body is far removed from this state of perfection, no matter how strongly the spirit of movement may be present in the would-be dancer, very little can be achieved.

The classical ballet is very demanding when it comes to the question of physical perfection. In character and national dancing, in the modern (contemporary) idiom of dancing, even in athletics, the demands are not so severe as in the world of classical ballet.

There is the problem of whether or not there is 'talent'. A dancer can have a perfect body and no talent. Yet it is a strange fact that this is seldom the case. Where there is perfect proportion in the physical sense there is, time and again, an inexplicable coordination of mind and body—some response to a law of which we know nothing.

We find it quite possible to recognise what type of dancer a student is going to be by the general physical outline. I have noted that a certain form of bone structure of the head and face produces complementary signs in the bone structure of leg and foot, and in the actual proportions of other parts of the body. These are facts that (with inevitable contradictions) crop up again and again and have become part of our daily observations. In the end we are bound to admit that it all leads to the axiom: the better the chosen dancer answers to the laws that rule a well-proportioned body, the better chance he stands to make a success of a career as a highly trained dancer.

There are failures, of course. Intelligence, musicality and character all play a sensitive yet positive part, and we have to remember that any wholly unimaginative approach to any form of physical perfection can be the most dangerous of all pastimes. As an example, physical perfection does not make anyone a first-class teacher, ballet master or choreographer.

Students take examinations and they pass. Any perfected form of teaching or study will enable them to do this, thus making things rather dangerously foolproof for them. Students may well absorb the theory without ever succeeding in turning their acquisition of knowledge to any real practical use. Acquired knowledge can be used well, badly or not at all.

All the arts are subject to laws of their own—laws that must be accepted—and many of them seem to be as much wrapped in mystery as the laws of the universe. They are there for all time. The art of movement is no exception. We know through the analysis of dance movement that the symmetry of the body responds to many laws. We have to learn not to break them, whether as dancers, teachers or choreographers.

The dance execution of a ballet dancer is as wonderful to analyse in theory as it is beautiful to look at in action. In preparation the training covers all those demands that nature permits to be made on the body when it reaches a higher plane of development and movement. Even here the limitations are set by the laws of nature. They must be recognised, for to overstrain the mechanism of the body is as serious as to overstrain the mechanism of the voice.

Most of our movements in life come to us naturally, through years of habit. A dancer, every day of his life when he dances, has to remain aware of movement, aware of the brain message to his body. The answer to that message amounts to a very important form of self-discipline and control, neither of which can ever be relaxed. The movement may be carefully memorised so that it can be repeated, but never can it be repeated without conscious attention to what is actually taking place.

Of course the possibility of injury is a very strong incentive to the development of a proper discipline. If a dance is executed carelessly, or an exercise incorrectly, an accident may occur. The other danger is that by continuous faulty movement a dancer may permanently alter the shape of his body or limbs. Thus dancers quickly acquire a highly developed sense of self-protection, and once that is very strongly developed they grasp the true meaning and significance of perfected detail.

It is common for the public to imagine that a dancer, once trained, has only to rehearse; that his years of study are over. This is not so: tuition goes on all the years of a dancing life.

No dancer can rehearse until he has had at least an hour and a half of practice every day. This is considered so important that there is a clause in the dancers' Equity contracts that compels a management to give no fewer than four lessons a week. Equity has, equally wisely, made it compulsory for the artist to attend these classes.

No artist worthy of the name would, of course, ever miss his classes. In fact, they all want more, and an organisation such as the Royal Ballet gives hours of tuition over and above the stated Equity minimum.

We have to give our dancers individual attention. In a large class all kinds of faults tend to creep into the work, and a dancer produces quite serious faults after a time. As an example, posture can go wrong through sheer fatigue. Or a peculiar pain in a boy's or girl's foot can be traced to a badly executed exercise. Sometimes a choreographic movement runs counter to the laws of movement in general—it may be unscientific and therefore harmful. Such lapses, when they occur, have to be detected and rectified.

Yet I always like to think of ballet as being the discipline of a very natural thing—ordinary, everyday movement, that is brought to a very great pitch of perfection. And if you discipline movement in this way you help to discipline your attitude to life.

The ballet teaches women dancers to mould themselves into some sort of visual perfection. I notice how little, in comparison, this seems to be developed in actresses. You recognise a dancer because there is an air of compact symmetry about her. It is true that some of this is due to her physical make-up; she is chosen so very carefully, and as I have said before, a well proportioned body has a habit of going with a well proportioned mental outlook. Thus women dancers manage to make more of their appearance than do other women in the theatre world. It is something they have learned to do to themselves. Instinctively they will never buy a dress that shows up the lines of the body to disadvantage. And if they make such mis-

193

takes, rest assured that they make the same mistakes in their work!

When I say dancer, I mean the many hundreds who are trained for the ballet in this country. I do not just refer to the stars—though it is the great stars that the general public tends to think of when the talk is of ballets and ballet dancers.

The theatre world goes through many phases, and there are signs that, particularly in opera and ballet, the star system is at present in the ascendant. Quite apart from the obvious reason—the particular talents of those artists who have gained and justly deserve international fame—there are tendencies not quite so praiseworthy.

Publicity is very often playing a disturbing role. Through radio, television and the press in general one can launch today, in a matter of weeks, a publicity campaign that, in the past, would have taken two years to handle, and modern travelling facilities enable a famous artist to keep a tenacious hold on his world-wide public.

The younger stars of the last few years are encountering a far more formidable task in establishing themselves, for they represent a second generation. As long as the first generation of stars is still with them in the same company, these new stars will have to meet competition with the past rather than with their own contemporaries. When, in the future, they take over, comparisons will be drawn.

Of course, a company like the Royal Ballet suffers rather less from the star system than most. It is accepted as a famous ensemble, and although names as always are an added attraction, the company itself has a very healthy following of its own. Most of its performances over the years are performances given by the regular artists of the Royal Ballet. There is in fact a rhythm in these things, more important than any frenzied controversy; in the final reckoning it can always be seen that great artists and great ensembles meet on common ground. You then find yourself asking the question about the hen and the egg ...

Even when it comes to careful planning for such an important thing as economic security for dancers, I can look back and see that nothing is the result just of planning. Circumstances thrust a lot on you, and when they arise you simply meet their demands.

It was the war that turned us from a struggling repertory theatre company into a prosperous commercial venture. It was the peace that gave us a great empty opera house and a sub-sidy—even if the subsidy at that time was really to open the doors of Covent Garden and to start an opera company. The Royal Ballet, known then as Sadler's Wells, simply walked in. And when the curtain went up it just found its own, much en-larged, faithful public packing the auditorium from floor to ceiling.

England has babbled for years about the dangers of national theatres, for we are past-masters at proving that half life's com-forts are not necessary. As with central heating, so with national theatres. For generations everything to do with art in this country has lived on charity, and we have developed a rather sentimental, happy-go-lucky attitude in consequence.

Of course there is the danger of a national theatre becoming over-institutionalised. It is a danger that has to be accepted. To admit such a possibility is surely the best way to combat it when the need arises.

The whole of the English theatre needs roots; its actors and actresses need them as much as singers and dancers—roots, moreover, from which they can if necessary break away. For the one form of experimental work that really succeeds is that which springs from a solid traditional background. The man who has not started to learn before he decides that he must un-learn may become a law unto himself for a short while. Yet his work may well fade into an example of arrested development or lawless delinquency.

I have always felt that when our public shake their heads in despair over the 'Establishment' (in other words the Royal Ballet) they are paying us a great compliment. For who would have thought that in such a short space of time we would be old enough, solid enough, tough enough and enough in the way to be debunked in so distinguished a fashion?

In such a theatre as the Royal Opera House we have had to face up to the fact that a public consisting of the 'regulars' is not enough. We have also to reach that vast and nomadic horde of people who come to see us only occasionally. These people visit us in the same spirit that they might visit the other theatres, with modest regularity or as a holiday treat for the younger generation. We have a duty to these tax-paying supporters of our work, and must hold ourselves responsible for their dose of culture along with their larger doses of fun.

III

I hope that I have by now made it clear that you cannot build up your company and your tradition entirely from the outside world. Indeed, I am quite certain that after the first process of assimilation a national theatre, be it drama or ballet, renews itself from within its own sources. The specialist from elsewhere is always welcome, yet it is only in perfectly run academic institutions that such people make a proper impact. Their knowledge takes the form of an evolution as it falls on soil fully prepared to receive it. We are, on such occasions, reminded of the parable of the sower.

In consequence teaching, in such an institution as the Royal Ballet School, has an immensely accumulative quality about it. You learn its theory, you study the principles of imparting this theory, and finally you sense how to teach. A good teacher must have great powers of observation. He cannot ever afford to be introspective. He must cultivate the power to project and understand how to meet the pupil further than halfway. A humourless teacher can fail, however knowledgeable. For to bore a pupil is infinitely worse than to give an unorthodox lesson.

Now that the Royal Ballet is so big it might appear that the pedagogy and the production sides can be two separate entities. This of course is not possible; the fusion is as subtle as it is all-important. The school has as many ex-members teaching as the ballet has ex-members directing.

*   *   *

I have digressed in this book in many directions. But directly or indirectly all the thoughts expressed, whether of today or yesterday, are linked with the history and evolution of an Establishment that bears the name of the Royal Ballet and the Royal Ballet School. I hope that its foundations and principles will stand up to the passage of time. I plead for a cool and tempered look into the future and a courageous summing-up of what the future asks of us. I would ask for those demands—that are reasoned and wise—to be met by all as both a duty and a worthwhile venture. A door ajar welcomes a draught, an open mind the world's fresh air.

EPILOGUE

DANCERS IN ACTION

(Dedicated to Kenneth MacMillan, choreographer, and to the dancers of the Royal Ballet in Mahler's Song of the Earth.*)*

They are filled with a quietude
And feel the dedication of their bodies
To movements that are self-contained.
Challenging all the formal laws of form,
And with a symmetry that quivers
Within its own acute awareness.
As a light wave is their golden glow
That warms the sluggish outline of those static forms
Who sit and watch with riveted attention.
Now this distant world falls into focus
As the extended curve of pattern reaches
To encroach on space where the dancers will
Transcend all earthbound earthiness.

The movement's peak is reached, and their return
Carries the speed and swoop of unhampered swallows,
While all earth's pressures wait to converge on
Lithe limb and brain and movement's ecstasy;
But their own world encases them,
And stillness reigns in that retreat
Where mind would scrutinise afresh,
Recalling that strange moment of great power
Which was the body's exploration of
A unity that this instant ceased to be.

N. de Valois

INDEX

200

202

203